From Garfield to Harding

From Garfield to Harding

The Success of Midwestern Front Porch Campaigns

Jeffrey Normand Bourdon

THE KENT STATE UNIVERSITY PRESS

Kent, Ohio

Contents

The Search for Dignity as a Candidate

The Changing Role of Presidential Contestants
in the Nineteenth Century

In the summer of 1888, Benjamin Harrison ran the first large-scale front porch campaign for the presidency from his home in Indianapolis, Indiana. The city of just over 32,000 saw more than 350,000 visitors, to whom Harrison delivered ninety-four speeches. The throngs came from all over the country by train and marched in colorful, exciting processions through town. Visitors were met by enthusiastic local crowds who joined them in backing the Republican candidate. When the delegations arrived at his home, a leader of the group would give a vetted speech and introduce Harrison. He would then greet the crowd, say something ingratiating about their history, and give issue-oriented speeches concerning tariff schedules, economic prosperity, and foreign policy. Following one of these virtuoso performances, the *Pittsburgh Dispatch* wrote something illuminating that the *Indianapolis Journal* later reprinted. The sheet pointed out that several recent presidential candidates had toured for the presidency and that Harrison's speeches were "in good taste. He scrupulously refrains from personalities. He fully comprehends the significance of the great issue at stake—protection—and rarely neglects to drive it home to the minds and consciences of his listeners. His style is plain and familiar, but his evident sincerity and wide acquaintance with the subject in hand give him an advantage possessed by few public speakers. He commands respect even when he fails to convince." The paper described

Harrison's conduct as admirable and predicted that, by November, the voters would know what a "full-fledged statesman" he was.[1]

The *Dispatch*'s assessment of Harrison's performance sheds light on the effectiveness of front porch campaigning for the presidency. Four Republicans tried the technique for the duration of their campaigns between 1880 and 1920: James Garfield in 1880, Harrison in 1888, William McKinley in 1896, and Warren Harding in 1920. They went undefeated. Front porch campaigning became popular at a time in presidential campaign history when actively seeking the office had not been effective. Candidates who went on speaking engagements had only been successful one time after five tours for the presidency between 1840 and 1872.[2]

The Founding Fathers' negative impression of seeking office seemed to loom over the campaign process during the nineteenth century. The first generation of American leaders lived out the adage, "the office seeks the man, not the other way around." Common thought held that stumping made candidates seem too aggressive, too interested in the office, and prone to the problems accompanying travel, such as poorly screened appearances and rowdy locals. In 1852 a canon malfunction killed a soldier while Winfield Scott was being introduced in Columbus, Ohio, during his tour as a Whig candidate. Eight years later a rally for Democrat Stephen Douglas in New York City turned into a food fight.[3] It also exposed candidates to unvetted moments and saw them give extemporaneous speeches that sometimes went wrong. In 1872 Democrat Horace Greeley lost his dignity by angering all of his audiences during his talks—whether they were northern or southern, black or white. By the 1880s candidates such as Garfield and Harrison did not want to seem disinterested in running, but they also did not want to come across as aggressive or unseemly. Front porch campaigning allowed them to connect with voters, make prepared statements that would be reprinted in newspapers across the country the next day, and maintain their dignity as candidates at a time when acceptable activity for a presidential contestant was a matter of debate. When the *Dispatch* described Harrison's style with such phrases as "commands respect," "good taste," "scrupulously refrains from personalities," "style is plain and familiar," "evident sincerity," and "full-fledged statesman," that was exactly what his handlers desired. Campaigning from the porch allowed him to appear interested in the office but not aggressively so. In its heyday, talking from the front porch proved to be a happy medium between aggressively stumping for the presidency and doing nothing to seek it. The strategy was also effective: no presidential candidate ever lost running from his porch.

Candidates who seemed sincere, plain, and familiar during the industrial era were accomplishing an important feat. Americans were seeing traditional, rural ideals give way to new, urban ideals as urbanization and demographic shifts served as natural outgrowths of industrialization. The process challenged almost every social norm, from the types of jobs available to workers to the ways that families functioned. Front porch campaigning allowed candidates to more actively run without breaking too far away from social and political customs. As the process unfolded, Republicans espoused a high tariff schedule to protect US factories, businesses, homes, and families; the position fit neatly with the delivery of their speeches from their homes. Industrialization catalyzed something called "impersonalization," in which workers and consumers had less individual contact with their bosses and storeowners—yet here were three presidential candidates willing to meet these same workers and consumers, give them a face-to-face talk from their porch, shake hands, and allow them to meet their families. Additionally, all four candidates were from Ohio, which gave them a more authentic, midwestern feel for visitors from the surrounding region.

Not only did front porch campaigning produce personable, somewhat active campaigns, but they also highlighted the vibrancy of several small, isolated, "island communities" in both Indiana and Ohio as the Midwest was being changed by industrialization. Mentor, Indianapolis, Canton, and Marion all provided a comfortable "Middle America" feel for visitors and served as a positive breath of rural America for many experiencing the downside of economic transformation. From the 1870s to the 1920s, many communities in the United States saw a dramatic shift in their value systems because of problems related to industrialization. Systems rooted in rural, agricultural, small-town values were giving away to systems couched in urban-oriented, bureaucratically minded, middle-class values. Front porch campaigns, particularly in 1888 and 1896, allowed two midwestern "island communities" to showcase themselves and show other "island communities" that they could still thrive. The process also saw growth throughout the Gilded Age. In 1880 Mentor, Ohio, only saw a few thousand visitors as front porch campaigning was still in its embryonic phase. Eight years later porch campaigning boomed as Indianapolis saw several hundred thousand visitors. In 1896 the process reached its apex in Canton, Ohio, when 750,000 people descended upon the small city. Finally, in 1920, Marion, Ohio, saw at least 250,000 visitors. The campaigns turned these relatively small communities into booming, thriving, exciting places whose extensive downtown areas offered further attractions for the party faithful. Many people in the Midwest were used to traveling for several hours by train to county and state fairs for a full day of exploration and pageantry. Taking a similarly long ride with the family to one of these campaign towns for a day of excitement paralleled that experience, making the process feasible for average citizens.[4]

The homebound style cemented Republicans as the party of home life, purity, and the protector of domestic, Christian ideals in the post–Civil War era.[5] The active role Garfield's wife took in interacting with visitors assisted the candidate, and the Republican Party, in painting themselves as sharers of their homes rather than masters of them—as Democrats were made to appear. During these years, the "ideal Democrat" was "an independent white man, master of his home, quick to defend his interests, and vigilant for signs of corrupt government power." Proper Democratic manhood meant uncontrolled male dominance. In contrast, Republicans wanted voters to know about their candidates' self-control through their domestic interactions. While Democratic men were "transformed by the moral influence of mothers, sisters, wives, and schoolteachers, in tribute to the maternal ideal."[6] For them, women helped men become the "masters" of their homes, and Republican men benefited from being the "sharers" of theirs with their wives and families. Front porch campaigning allowed Republican candidates to live up to this gendered ideal in a public way for the highest office in the land.

Despite the relative isolation of the midwestern towns, the folksy message and symbolism of the front porch campaigns became a vital part of the partisan, daily, national news cycle. Highly Republican newspapers consistently printed the candidates' speeches throughout all four campaigns. The orations were printed as close to verbatim as possible and almost always included an analysis of the nature of the crowds and the candidates' interactions with them. Small and large partisan papers from around the country had a tendency to carry the same cohesive story. Pro-Republican sheets of this sort included the *Chicago Tribune,* the *New York Tribune,* the *Cleveland Herald,* and the *Springfield (Massachusetts) Republican.* Papers such as the *Cleveland Plain Dealer,* the *Washington Post,* and the *Saint Louis Dispatch* offered more critical views of the four campaigns. The *New York Herald* went from being a pro-Republican paper in 1880 to a pro-Democratic organ by 1888 and covered the last three porch campaigns more critically. The *Painesville Telegraph* supported their local hero, Garfield, in 1880 and apparently did not have any negative stories to report. Local Indianapolis papers, such as the *Sun,* did mention more riffraff activity in 1888 while still supporting Harrison.

In 1896 and 1920 the *Canton Repository* and the *Marion Star* also included some negative stories about happenings in town but still wholeheartedly supported their respective local son's porch campaign. Overall, the process helped unify Republicans on a national level behind strong, outspoken candidates, especially by 1888 and 1896, when the porch campaigns became much larger. It also probably contributed to their victories in those years. In 1880 and 1888 Republican sheets were reprinting the candidates' speeches and interactions, while their Democratic opponents gave no speeches and had no interactions with the voters that their papers could report. In 1896 and 1920 Republican papers were able to reprint the complete speeches of their hopefuls, while Democratic reporters were forced to follow their candidates orating from a caboose while trying to copy down their speeches as accurately as possible. The Republican efforts created a message that proved to be unified, clear, and accurate.

The Gilded Age and the Progressive Era also saw the federal government become a modern institution as it became more centralized and responsive to citizens' needs. Front porch campaigning mirrored this change because it helped Republicans more effectively centralize themselves around presidential candidates with messages promising to help people. The process took a long time, starting with John C. Frémont in 1856 and Abraham Lincoln in 1860, and culminated with the presidency of Theodore Roosevelt during the first decade of the twentieth century. The campaigns in 1880, 1888, and 1896 each contributed to this party centralization in a different way. Garfield's effort started the process in 1880 through the newspaper coverage of his talks. Throughout his speeches, the candidate mixed historical symbolism with promises to help meet his supporter's needs; his rhetoric was carried nationally. In 1888 and 1896 Republican supporters from around the country could read about voters from their state and local city visiting their party's presidential candidates and interacting with them. In 1920 Harding repeated the process on a slightly smaller scale. The last three porch campaigns also saw Republican campaign managers and organizers on the local, state, and national level collaborate, organize, and orchestrate the crowds, the message, and the dissemination of the speeches nationally. Front porch campaigning helped Republicans centralize themselves nationally behind candidates that appeared popular, folksy, and somewhat issue oriented. It also forced party managers from the national, state, and local levels to work together to present a cohesive message from a strong candidate that not only kept Republicans together but also brought some new voters into their fold.

When the visitors arrived, they experienced a different style of politicking than they were used to. Front porch campaigning saw Republicans shift from the spectacle style that had been employed for over half a century to the newly popular, educational style. By the 1820s almost all white men could vote, so Democrats, and eventually Whigs, decided that the best way to garner the most support was to entertain voters with parades, alcohol, fiery speeches, and as much hoopla as possible. William Henry Harrison's tour in 1840 and Scott's talks in 1852 were attempts at an unusual form of spectacle campaigning: allowing voters to actually hear and interact with the major-party candidate himself. In the 1880s both parties started focusing on a calmer, more sterile form of spreading their message: educational campaigns.[7] In theory, this meant putting down the alcohol and calmly learning about the issues and the philosophies of the candidates. In reality, on the national level, it meant combining spectacle and educational styles. The parades to the candidate's home provided the spectacle, while the man's speeches provided education on the issues to the voters. Harrison and his campaign managers started combining the two styles in 1888, and eight years later McKinley perfected the process.

As spectacle politics gave away to the educational style, technological advances also changed how Republicans branded their candidates' messages and campaign events. While industrialization spawned several new developments in the ways that businesses advertised their products to growing numbers of consumers, front porch campaigning offered Republicans the opportunity to mirror these effective practices by perfecting the art of merchandising a product—the candidate and his life story playing out on the front porch—and effectively selling it to voters through newspapers. Garfield ran before brands really existed, although his supporters started the process by making local events on his front porch known to a national audience. By 1888 branding was developing in the economy, and Harrison's campaigners were merchandising their candidate in many different ways. Philadelphia business magnate John Wannamaker was an important organizer for Republicans that year. The party became so cagey at branding that voters were able to read its newspapers and learn about Harrison's shoe size, pant size, and head size. They could even read about what kind of underwear he preferred alongside his aspirations for a high tariff. Republicans took the process further in 1896 with more newspapers, more advertising, and a touring opponent who they could brand against by making him seem like an inexperienced hayseed. By 1920 Harding's background as a newspaper editor and his continued personal relationships with other editors both helped his advertising cause in the press. The Republicans' skillset at merchandising their candidate through newspapers helped a very unlikely candidate in early 1920 win over 60 percent of the popular vote later that fall. While Democrats were able to brand their candidates to a degree, front porch campaigning allowed Republicans to do this in a more personalized, in-depth, complex way that paved the way to electoral success.

While porch campaigning allowed Republicans to cozy up to white male voters, it also saw them act like they cared about other visitors, such as women, African Americans, naturalized citizens, and foreign visitors. All four candidates paid lip service to these groups from their porches and then effected no, or little, legislation on their behalf as president. While campaigning, they used their wives and children strategically to reach out to women and family-oriented men, ensuring that they were consistently visible in the audiences for the talks and then in the homes afterward. The three Gilded Age candidates always made sure women knew that their stance on the high protective tariff had everything to do with safeguarding American families. African Americans and naturalized voters also participated in all four front porch campaigns. All four as candidates offered platitudes to both groups, while the onset of Jim Crow segregation in the South and a series of federal, anti-immigration quota laws were put into place during their administrations. Despite all of the failed promises and lack of legislative help for these groups, by 1920, Harding's managers were still insisting on holding a "Colored Voters Day" and a "Foreign Voters Day." Harding himself begged women from his porch not to vote against male Republican congressional candidates who had opposed female suffrage in previous years.

Besides those groups, the candidates also saw Civil War Union veterans. Garfield and Harrison were both Union generals and received visitors who claimed to have fought with them on battlefields; McKinley had served first in the ranks, then as a junior officer. Here, too, the candidates' style synthesized well with their message for this group. Campaigning from their porches, these men promised to protect the pensions of fellow Union veterans as a means to protect their families and homes. Republicans were proud of their political and military heritage—many of them enjoyed linking the memory of Civil War with the rise of their party. The fact that Garfield, Harrison, and McKinley had participated in the war made their porch campaigns the perfect theaters for such celebrations of memory, efforts particularly important for the pride of Union soldiers. By the 1880s reconciliation activities and reunion marches with Confederate veterans were beginning to take place. These events sometimes did not sit well with some former Union soldiers who felt that their victory was being tainted by such ceremonies. The ability to march to a former commander's home and gather together to hear him speak about important issues helped reassert the pride of these veterans as well as their sense of masculinity in public. Seven survivors from Ulysses S. Grant's original regiment even brought a "tattered old battle-flag," which they flew while fighting under him, to Harrison in 1888.[8]

The battle flag presentation was part of an ever-changing process on the front porch campaign trail: gift exchange. These exchanges happened as part of a two-way process. Visitors often left Garfield's farm, for example, with apples from his orchards or vegetables from his fields. By 1888 visitors were bringing gifts to Harrison, including a five-hundred-pound piece of ore from Vermillion Range miners, a gigantic eagle from Colorado, a plush chair that represented the presidential chair, as well as canes, watermelons, and produce from their own farms.[9] Harrison accepted all of the gifts, from the normal to the zany, with a smile and a handshake for the presenters. McKinley also received a series of unusual gifts, including the black horse he rode in Chicago when he represented Ohio in the world's fair in 1893. Harding received an occasional gift in 1920, such as a headdress from a group of Native Americans, but his campaign saw fewer exchanges than his two Republican predecessors. Exchanging gifts helped candidates interact with voters and leave them with a positive memory to tell (and an occasional souvenir to show) a friend.

Handshaking also helped voters meet and connect with the candidates personally. Garfield shook hands with a few thousand voters in Mentor. Eight years later Harrison's campaign attracted 350,000 visitors, and he insisted on shaking hands with as many of them as possible. He bragged that he could shake sixty hands per minute and tried to squeeze the hand of each newcomer first so they would not shake his own too tightly. Newspapers claimed that the activity made him either more personable or ridiculous looking, with one labeling the handshaking as Harrison's "pump handle exercises." In 1896 McKinley's stenographer actually stuck his arm under the candidate's to shake the hand of an onrushing drunk.[10] By 1920 there seemed to be little debate: Harding needed to shake as many hands as possible. Newspaper coverage of the gift giving and handshaking provided plenty of fodder to Republican sheets looking to brand there candidates as "dignified," "personable," and "family-oriented."

Although successful in its heyday, a combination of factors led to the demise of running from the porch. In 1908 Republican William Taft started a front porch campaign in Cincinnati but eventually decided to change strategy and stump. The rise of Teddy Roosevelt and William Bryan as amazing stump speakers, the ubiquity of Progressivism at the turn of the century, the birth of modern advertising, the personalities of Republican candidates Calvin Coolidge and Herbert Hoover in the 1920s, and larger historical circumstances—the Great Depression in the 1930s and World War II in the 1940s—all combined to end the attractiveness and practicality of this style of politics. But while it was alive, front porch campaigning never resulted in a loss for a Republican candidate and always saw excited visiting crowds mingling with vociferous locals.

CHAPTER I

Germans, Jubilee Singers, and Axe Men

James A. Garfield and the Original Front Porch
Campaign for the Presidency

James A. Garfield sometimes had a flair for the dramatic as a presidential candidate in the campaign of 1880. No previous contestant had ever openly invited groups of people to visit him at his residence, but that is exactly what Garfield did in the summer of 1880. As the first front porch campaign in American history unfolded, personal friends, unknown well-wishers, and different groups all traveled to Mentor, Ohio, and visited him at his Lawnfield home. The visits ranged from the mundane to the dramatic. On October 1, 1880, the Jubilee Club from Fisk College was about to fulfill an obligation in Painesville, Ohio, and decided to stop at Lawnfield. They gathered in Garfield's living room, which his personal secretary, Joseph Stanley-Brown, later described as "big" and "well-filled." As Garfield walked by his secretary on his way into the room, he said, "My boy! I am going to say a word to them if it kills me." Realizing that there were no reporters to record the potentially dramatic event, Stanley-Brown wrote down all the events he witnessed in a notebook. The club's leader gave an "effecting speech" before the group started singing African American spirituals, at which people watching became "increasingly emotional." Stanley-Brown wrote that "tears were trickling down the cheeks of many of the women, and one staid old man blubbered audibly behind a door." Once the singers were done, Garfield rose and, "standing at ease besides the fireplace with his hand resting lightly on the mantle," he began talking to the crowd in "low conversational tones" and employed "rhetorical periods," which southerners in his audience would be able to appreciate. According to Stanley-Brown, the candidate said that he understood the needs and desires of a "race out of place" and finished his talk with "clear, ringing tones": "And I tell you now, in the closing days of this campaign, that I would rather be with you defeated than against you and victorious." Immediately following Garfield's remarks, according to his secretary, there was a moment of complete silence followed by the sound of "human expirations in unison." The story of the event appeared in newspapers in Cleveland, but Garfield's closing statements were omitted from the reports.[1] No matter how this event was reported, Garfield's front porch campaign undoubtedly produced some unique and dramatic moments like the interlude with the Jubilee Club.

Maybe most importantly, it does not appear that Garfield offended anybody during the contest. He actually proved to be one of the more active presidential candidates in the nineteenth century as he conducted a front porch campaign, spoke at three military gatherings, kept up correspondence with his political backers, and managed to go on a stump-speaking tour by train to New York State in early August. Onlookers contrasted this active campaign style with the inactivity of the Democratic candidate, Winfield Hancock, who did not tour or speak to groups of voters at his home. The porch not only gave Garfield a public voice but also made him seem much more in touch with common men than his seemingly aloof opponent. A campaign style that featured the candidate as the front man of the party also helped Republicans continue the process of unifying their party behind a strong presidential candidate. In what became the closest popular vote in American presidential history, the homebound effort certainly played a role in the party's victory.[2]

Garfield started the first front porch campaign because he simply did not want to upset his friends and prospective voters: "I could not play dummy on my own doorstep, when my yard was filled with voters from all parts of the country, hurling speeches at me on all subjects."[3] Once he had said yes to a visit from one group of friends or small club of people, it became very difficult to say no to another. The crowds themselves helped catalyze his efforts by simply showing up at his home. The process snowballed until it became an integral part of the candidate's strategy. There is no evidence that the Republican Party's national chairman, business merchant Marshall Jewel, either criticized or supported Garfield's decision to try this novel campaign technique. In 1876 Rutherford Hayes did not actively campaign and was sometimes mocked for it in the press. When Hayes lost the popular vote, one sheet contended that Republicans had "blundered . . . in making too much of the party and too little of the candidate and his principles."[4] Lawnfield provided a venue for Garfield to show and explain his principles to voters. The effort served both the candidate and his party in a multitude of ways. Garfield's homebound tactics allowed him to perform three individual campaign functions: (1) meet prospective voters and make them feel comfortable in his home, (2) invite important Republican leaders to his house to conduct critical backroom meetings under the guise of the "front porch" style, and (3) keep up with his correspondence. It also allowed the Ohioan to publicly present himself as the Republican nominee when powerful party members like James Blaine and Roscoe Conkling overshadowed him on the national stage. Visitors could be put into four categories: personal friends from the past, well-wishing acquaintances, Republican political leaders, and "deputations," or specific organizations that came in groups.

The front porch campaign developed in three phases. During phase one, friends, well-wishers, and acquaintances in small groups visited Garfield after his acceptance of the Republican nomination from mid-July to early September 1880. Phase two lasted five weeks, beginning on September 4, when occasional large groups, interspersed with small groups and individuals, visited the candidate. The turning point came when Republicans won state elections in Ohio and Indiana on October 12 and 13, and people began to realize that they had the opportunity to see the presidential frontrunner in his own home. From October 15 to 31, groups of hundreds and sometimes thousands descended upon Lawnfield as phase three unfolded. This final part of the process saw Garfield's homebound effort turn into the type of spectacle politics that many political observers had grown used to for half a century.[5] The events that took place in Mentor in September and October were reported throughout the country in newspapers. Republican sheets carried the speeches that the candidate gave, reported on the parades that the delegations made to his farm, and detailed the interactions that visitors had with Garfield and his family. These events helped Republicans portray him as a down-to-earth, understanding family man who was well aware of the needs and desires of the people he encountered. Suddenly, on November 1, the process ended as abruptly as it started.

The issues facing presidential candidates fluctuated as politics in the 1870s saw white voters become less concerned about African Americans in the South and more interested in matters related to industrialization, corruption in government, and the spoils system. The Republican Party itself was divided into three groups over the spoils system and the use of political patronage, support for the Grant administration, and advocacy for Radical Reconstruc-tion. A faction within the party calling themselves Stalwarts supported Grant throughout his scandal-plagued administration, backed the continuation of Radical Reconstruction, and thought that Republicans should actively use political patronage to support party leaders and the party faithful. Popular partisan leaders, such as Conkling and John Sherman, as well as lesser-known men like Chester Arthur, led this group. Another group within the party, called Half-Breeds (a name invented by Stalwarts as a pejorative characterization of those perceived as not fully committed Republicans) and spearheaded by Blaine, remained only partially loyal to Grant, supported civil-service reform, and backed a merit system for federal employment. Led by Carl Schurz, a third group, called the Independents, wanted a massive overhaul of the civil-service system. Going into the convention, the Republicans knew that the unpopular President Hayes would not be seeking a second term, so the Conkling-led Stalwarts favored a third term for Grant. The former president held a slight lead at the beginning of the convention over party leaders and Half-Breeds Blaine and Sherman. But after days of nothing but deadlock and gridlock among bickering faction leaders, Wisconsin delegates switched their votes over to Garfield, beginning the complicated process of building support for him. After thirty-six votes were taken, Garfield at last secured the nomination.[6] The candidate himself identified with the Half-Breeds, so Republican leaders chose Arthur as his vice presidential running mate as a concession to the Stalwarts. With his party divided over issues and the nomination, Garfield knew he had his work cut out for him if he wanted to win the general election. It was from this backdrop that the candidate had to figure out how to campaign for the presidency against Democrat Hancock.

Despite the factionalism within the Republican Party, Garfield had a solid history as a general and congressman from Ohio. The last of seven log-cabin presidents, Garfield was born into modest means to a widowed mother, who he remained close to for the rest of his life. He worked as a carpenter to finance his education and in 1856 graduated from Williams College in Mas-sachusetts. Following school, Garfield became a Republican and campaigned against slavery in Ohio. In 1858 he married Lucretia Rudolph and became an Ohio state senator a year later. Garfield opposed secession and in 1861 and 1862 served as a brigadier general in the Union army, fighting in battles like Middle Creek, Shiloh, and Chickamauga. A year later he was selected to be the member of the US House of Representatives from Ohio's Nineteenth Dis-trict. For the next seventeen years, he worked as a member of the House and earned a reputation as a skilled orator who supported civil-service reform, a bimetal monetary system, agricultural technology, an educated citizenry, and a relatively moderate approach to civil rights. By 1880 Garfield had chaired three committees in the House.[7] It was from this position that he received the Republican Party's nomination for the presidency, which he formally accepted on July 10, 1880.

Not only did Garfield have a nice political and military résumé, but he also cast a striking physical figure. James D. McCabe described him as "six feet high, broad shouldered, and strongly built," having "an unusually large head, that seems to be three-fourths forehead, light brown hair and beard, large light blue eyes, a prominent nose and full cheeks." Another biographer characterized Garfield's head as "massive" and his brain as "gigantic." He weighed approximately 240 pounds. It appears as though Garfield never took to luxurious dress or living either: "He dresses plainly, is fond of broad-brimmed slouch hats and stout boots, eats heartily, [and] cares nothing for luxurious living." McCabe also stressed that the candidate was an intellectual family man who seemed perfectly comfortable staying at home, writing that he was "thoroughly temperate in all respects save in that of brain work, and is devoted to his wife and children, and very fond of his country home." Garfield had an affinity for using nicknames, actually calling one young son "Dutch Brig" and the other "Little Yacht" because he was always fond of the military and the sea. He called his wife "Squirrel" and his daughter "Scuti-fer." His secretary and telegraph operator, Stanley-Brown, was known as the "Hurler of Lightning," or sometimes just "Hurler." Probably Garfield's best nickname was saved for his Newfoundland dog; after a particularly frustrating year in Congress in 1879, he gave the dog the nickname "Veto." Beyond this, McCabe asserted of the Ohioan, "Among men he is genial, approachable, companionable, and a remarkably entertaining talker." Garfield has also been described as "charming" and possessing "unpretentious politeness for which he is distinguished."[8] With this type of physical and personal description, the candidate certainly had the tools to meet with prospective voters. But with the recent failures of presidential hopefuls Horatio Seymour and Horace Greeley from the stump, it was doubtful that he would be making extensive speaking tours for the presidency.

Garfield was also positively described by his neighbors in Mentor, who never thought of him as "proud" or "stuck up . . . although they thought he might become so when he first moved among them." His wife was described as a "perfect lady" who was not afraid to do work, while his mother was "an intelligent, energetic old lady, with a clear head and a strong will, who keeps well posted on the news of the day, and is very proud of her son's career, though more liberal of criticism than praise." Garfield's two living sons attended college in New Hampshire during the campaign season, but his daughter, Molly, a "handsome, rosy cheeked girl of about twelve," and two younger sons were still living in Mentor with the family. Sometimes Garfield liked to play tennis or croquet with his daughter or other family members. At dinner the family went through each individual entry in a "little Dictionary of three thousand words" because Garfield did not want the conversation to constantly revolve around the presidential race.[9] The appearance of a pretty daughter and two younger sons at the home of the candidate could have only helped his image as a man capable of understanding the problems that families faced due to industrialization, a president who (along with his party) championed home life and would strive to protect domestic tranquility. These images combined to help the campaign merchandise Garfield as a man still immersed in Jeffersonian ideals despite society's shift to more Hamiltonian ones.

Corydon Fuller's visit to Lawnfield provides a vivid picture of the personable nature of the front porch campaign and its connection to the Jeffersonian ideal. An old friend of Garfield's, Fuller visited him in the summer of 1880. He arrived at Lawnfield at ten o'clock in the morning and found Garfield dictating letters to his two stenographers. The guest noted that in one corner of the room was a pile of newspapers so high that they could fill a "large wagon-box," along with approximately 5,000 letters and telegrams piled about the floor. Garfield gave some "rapid directions" to his assistants and then took his friend by carriage around the farm. Fuller claimed that the candidate "had not desired the nomination that he had received, at the present time, but would have preferred to spend a few years in the Senate. He said he did not deny to hope at some future time to receive it, after he had become better prepared to execute its great duties; but as it had come unsought, he should accept, and if elected, do the best he could." Garfield pointed out the changes and improvements he had made around the farm in recent years, especially an orchard that he had planted. He also stopped the carriage for a moment to speak to his foreman about some hay that needed to be moved. When the two men returned to the house, Garfield summoned a hired man to put the horses up and invited Fuller inside for dinner. The friends entered the kitchen, where Garfield's mother was apparently pitting cherries to put into a pie for dessert. Fuller claimed that as they approached her, Garfield asked if he knew "this little old woman" and "affectionately" laid his hand on her shoulder. He then added, "Mother, don't you remember Corydon?" Mrs. Garfield then gave Fuller a "cordial greeting" as the two men passed into another room.[10] This interlude also illuminates the symbolism of small-town values that Garfield's homestead was capable of exuding.

While the majority of the larger group visits to Lawnfield did not really pick up until October, according to one Garfield biographer, the first "considerable" group came to the home on September 4. After "a company of ninety-five ladies and gentlemen from Indiana arrived by special train, having walked to the house from the railroad by way of the lane," as Garfield identified them, he appeared in front of them. The *Painesville Telegraph* explained that the special train contained three cars that "were handsomely decorated with flags and banners and pictures of Garfield." The group "marched throughout" the fields surrounding the home and were "pleasantly and cordially welcomed" by the family. The *Indianapolis Journal* characterized the group as "a very intelligent company, representing every leading branch of commercial business." Garfield admitted that he was expecting their visit, having received advance notice, but added, "I am very pleasantly surprised at the large number of ladies and gentlemen who have honored me by this visit." He described the "magical powers" of American labor, internal trade, and the advances of the Western Reserve (the Midwest) for the last eighty-four years. Garfield delved into a detailed history of the settlement of Indiana and explained that it was a prime example of American ingenuity and hard work. The candidate noted that in 1796 a group of forty-two surveyors had landed in the area that was later named Indiana: "At that time from the Pennsylvania line to Detroit hardly a smoke ascended from the white man's cabin." But in 1880, he pointed out, "the Western Reserve furnishes happy and comfortable homes to more than three-fourths of a million intelligent people."[11] These remarks helped establish two trends for Garfield at home: he always made broad pronouncements that were uncontroversial, and he personally identified with each audience.

Following this event, Garfield talked with the chairman of the group, George Webster, declaring that he was highly pleased with the call and that such visits "were just what he wanted made, but not what he expected." According to the *Indianapolis Journal,* after the speech the visitors were invited to meet the candidate, his wife, and his mother. The group also formed a glee club, which sang several patriotic songs for the family. Two days after the visit, the *Journal* complimented the candidate for his stellar performance: "Garfield's speech to the commercial travelers . . . must have classed among his happiest efforts in this line of speaking. He possesses in a remarkable degree the art of saying the right thing in the right way. He is always appropriate . . . and never commonplace. . . . They show him to be a man of great, varied, and ready resources." The *Painesville Telegraph* also lauded the event, contending that the call "was perhaps one of the most pleasant and agreeable made at the General's residence since his nomination." Its report claimed that members of both political parties were in attendance so that the meeting was "devoid of political significance" and was more than a "straw" because members of both parties held Garfield in such "high esteem." When the throng left, the paper opined, they were "all well pleased with their courteous reception." While the *Telegraph* may have surmised that the meeting was "devoid of political significance," with the visit of ninety-five Indianans, the second phase of the front porch campaign had begun. By visiting Garfield, his audience gave him a public platform that he made sure to use to his political advantage, even if the group did not know that they were acting politically. Garfield was also aware that Indiana would be a key swing state in the upcoming contest. The talks he gave to the visitors may have had a substantive influence on the election, for Garfield won the popular vote in Indiana by just over 1 percent, thus securing all fifteen of the state's Electoral College votes.[12] Reports of this meeting may have convinced some Hoosier voters to pick him.

Recently, historians have stressed the intricate organization of the front porch campaigns of Harrison and McKinley. They have also argued that the candidates made direct statements about issues: in Harrison's case the high protective tariff, new laws for railroad safety, and the ability of labor to arbitrate; and in McKinley's speeches the gold standard and the tariff.[13] Garfield's style differed from his successors. He never made precise statements about issues related to the political economy, such as protective tariffs, labor-protection laws, or the gold standard, nor did he really engage in educational campaigning from his porch. Yet Garfield always made positive pronouncements in front of German and Irish American visitors, African Americans, and groups of women. In addition, whenever the candidate spoke to a regional group, he commented favorably about their region and its history. Also, when he spoke to different types of labor groups, he always spoke in ways that would endear him to them. Garfield made sure that he ingratiated himself to each group by personalizing his talk to champion their interests without taking precise stances on critical issues that his opponents could take apart. While these speeches may have come off in the newspapers as hollow and transparent, his words were actually carefully chosen as he pursued his goals to make people feel comfortable at his home, to recognize them as individuals and important groups, and to avoid saying anything that would give his opponents political ammunition. It was promotion, or advertising, politics.

Garfield's precision from the porch contrasted starkly with his opponent's lack of efficiency. Hancock did not actively campaign, some even claiming that he was incapable of such efforts. One satirist wrote that the candidate pretended to faint when two rival Democratic groups visited him at the same time, allegedly stating afterward, "There must be a new plan fixed. . . . I can't keep on faintin' in this way till the first uv November." As an *Indianapolis Journal* reporter put it: "Not only has he no political experience; he has no political principles, so far as I know. He simply wants to be president." Republican editors simultaneously attacked the candidate's military record and his masculinity by positing that he had been of little use during the Battle of Gettysburg, was cruel to his soldiers, and wore a corset under his outfit. They claimed that he had "pretty-man ideas in dress" and had evolved into a "self-maid man." Hancock explained, "I have no right to mar the present situation of the party by a set of expressions, superfluous to its adopted platform of principles, with which I am in full accord." Yet when the Democrat decided to break his silence, he gaffed when speaking to the press on a key issue—the tariff. In an interview with the *Paterson Daily Guardian,* he contended that the "tariff question was a local question" and that "the general government seldom cares to interfere" in the tariff debate. Hancock quickly realized that his statements made him seem uneducated on the realities of the subject, so he did another interview in which he proclaimed that he was "too sound an American to advocate any departure from the general features of a policy that has been largely instrumental in building up our industries and keeping Americans from the competition of the underpaid labor of Europe." These statements underscored the importance of the tariff issue in 1880, but they also exposed Hancock's inexperience as a candidate in contrast with Garfield's string of mistake-free speeches. One Republican onlooker laughingly stated, "That, is one interview too many." Democratic National Party chairman William H. Barnum blamed Hancock's loss on the interview; Barnum believed that talking could only hurt a candidate's bid.[14] The Democratic press never had a chance to brand their candidate for potential voters like the front porch campaign allowed their opponents to do for their own. While the Republican nominee appeared candid, personable, and affable in the press, his Democratic counterpart seemed aloof, inexperienced, unknowledgeable, and even unmasculine.

In late September and early October, the crowds visiting Mentor increased as the second phase reached its apex. On September 28 President Grant, Senator Conkling, Rep. Levi Morton, and Sen. John Logan came to Lawnfield in a "hack-like vehicle" and were escorted by "two mounted squadrons of Garfield Guards," who had torches that produced "considerable light." The men had an informal conversation and an "elegant" lunch with Garfield and his family.[15] The *Painesville Telegraph* described the meeting as "warm and cordial." When Garfield and Conkling met, the candidate said in a "hospitable way" to the New Yorker, "Senator, I am indeed glad to see you." Conkling responded, "General, I am very glad to see you in your own home." The *Telegraph* posited that it was "especially notable that their hand clasp was strong and that the words spoken were spontaneous from the heart."[16] The candidate then took the four men to his front porch and introduced them to two hundred visitors waiting on his lawn. According to Garfield, "each made a courteous remark, but no speech."[17]

Grant and Conkling's visit to Mentor became the first major event of the campaign. Following all of the consternation at the Republican convention in June, party leaders needed to show a unified front to both loyal backers and undecided voters. This meeting generated goodwill between Conkling and Garfield and helped break the frequently icy relationship between the two men. While many Republican leaders remained divided into Stalwarts and Half-Breeds, the top party leaders needed to make a public truce. Garfield had garnered the nomination for the presidency, but he knew that he needed to mend the political fence with the large, powerful faction of Stalwarts within the Republican Party. But Stalwarts like Conkling knew that, while they may not see eye to eye with Garfield on issues like the use of the spoils system, it would still be politically expedient to publicly unify with the party's presidential candidate during an election year. Lawnfield, already the site of a growing front porch campaign, served as the perfect location for such an important public meeting. The Republican press started referring to the meeting as the "Treaty at Mentor" following the strife at the convention.[18] It was an event designed to be disseminated around the United States to let voters know that the Republican leadership was consolidated and united behind a strong candidate.

Several more groups visited Lawnfield at the very end of September and early October. The Jubilee Club from Nashville came on September 30. On October 8 the Young Men's First Voters Garfield and Arthur Club from Cleveland visited. According to Garfield, this group numbered four hundred and came by a special six-car train. Led to Lawnfield by a "band of music," the men were all young Republicans who were about to cast their vote in a presidential election for the first time. The club's president, Herman W. Grannis, briefly introduced Garfield, who then delivered a "happy speech" in which he declared that he had never heard of such a large group of young men, about to struggle with the "great questions of their history," making such a visit: "I know of nothing quite like this in our history." Garfield noted that he was a "little disenchanted" because he was not part of the group himself, having always considered himself a young man, and admitted that he must be an old man because he had cast his first vote for president before any in his audience had been born; his joke was met with laughter and applause. Garfield even told the men that he sometimes felt like Rip Van Winkle awakening from his sleep and occasionally having to ask, "Who in the world am I?" After this he became much more serious and discussed the importance of buying domestically made products instead of name items from foreign places. The candidate pointed out that, while he was in school, he and his classmates had whittled their own pencils, which they always found to be better than any pencils that any classmate bought from abroad. Any classmate could acquire a handful of homemade pencils for the price of a "boughton" pencil, he claimed, yet every one of the homemade specimens was better. Garfield warned the young men not to suffer from these types of "delusions," as he called them. The general also expounded on a fear that all Republicans expressed: Democrats stuffing the ballot box on Election Day. Garfield told his listeners, "When I see such a band of earnest young men as meet me here today I feel certain that if they could deploy themselves as ballot box guard . . . such defenders will keep the Republic pure and keep it free." Aware of the bucolic setting that his home provided, the candidate emphasized it in closing: "The house is small, the farm is small, the township is small, the county is a small one, but all there is in it to give of generosity and hospitality and welcome that is in my hands to give, is yours while you stay." The end of Garfield's talk was met with "applause and cheers," the candidate clearly having connected with his audience. His rhetoric also demonstrated a keen awareness of the ambience that his farm as an "island community" gave off to visitors.[19]

Importantly, homebound efforts allowed Garfield and his Republican successors to reach out to first-time voters and personally incorporate them into their campaigns. Between 1880 and 1896, approximately 74–79 percent of all eligible voters participated in presidential elections, most of which were extremely close. Many older voters already knew who they were supporting before the contests even began because partisan passions ran so high. One analyst has estimated that during the Gilded Age, "at least" 90 percent of midwesterners were firmly committed Democrats or Republicans.[20] This made selling the partisan brand to first-time voters critical for any candidate trying to make enough of a dent in the electorate to pull out a close contest. Republican presidential hopefuls of this period personally met young voters and made them feel welcome to their homes, something not offered by the Democratic candidate in 1880 or 1888. In such close contests, these interludes may have been the most important for building winning coalitions.

A day after the visit from the Young Men's Club, the "last grand rally of Republicans" came to Lawnfield. The *Painesville Telegraph* claimed that participants numbered between ten thousand and twelve thousand people from the Ohio towns of Madison, Perry, and Painesville, identifying one group as the "Boys in Blue" and another as the Madison Glee Club. The procession carried a sign with a picture of a factory in full operation with the phrases "Protective Tariff," "Wanted, 100 men," and "high wages" inscribed on its wall. On the flip side was a picture of a closed factory, over which was a message reading "Tariff for Revenue Only" and underneath "Pauper Wages," and a mechanic headed to Omaha while his wife and children cry. In a "grand and imposing spectacle," the crowd marched by Garfield's home, where the candidate greeted them from the front porch. The paper also noted that every township in Lake County was represented.[21] October 9 proved to be the apex of the second phase of Garfield's homebound effort, which sought to consistently produce events for newspapers to report and for voters to consume.

Early in the first porch effort, Republican strategists started weighing the importance of the tariff in the campaign more heavily because of the outcomes of state elections in Maine in mid-September. Republicans did well in manufacturing towns but not shipping towns, which showed them how much traction the issue had. Leaders in the party had come out of their convention thinking that the southern question would be paramount in the contest, but now they were convinced that the tariff was the key to shoring up northern states—none of which they could lose in a close race.[22] While Garfield would remain relatively ambiguous about the topic in his speeches from home, he would certainly be making some references to tariffs for his visitors.

The workers arriving from Perry, Madison, and Painesville may have experienced harsh, impersonal conditions at their jobs, but the front porch campaign allowed them personal access to a candidate who seemed able to identify with them and their plights. Garfield's support for a high protective tariff also went hand in hand with his campaign style. The tariff protected domestically manufactured products, prices, and wages, which meant that it directly affected workers' jobs, families, and homes; complimentary, the front-porch campaign provided the opportunity for workers to enter into Garfield's home, meet his family, and receive a personal assurance that their livelihoods would be protected by a Republican president.[23] This further helped Republicans paint themselves as the party of protection over the home by making a pragmatic economic argument.[24] They also employed sexual references to illustrate their protection policy. Did workingmen want to see their pregnant wives employed in brothels to make the money needed to raise their children in a free-trade economy? The mantle of protection proved important to assume in 1880 because, throughout the ensuing decade, national political leaders and movements would increasingly sell their brand based on what they could do to help people's homes and families.[25]

Republican leaders were also aware that the outcomes of state congressional elections in Ohio and Indiana in October would most likely foreshadow the presidential-election results in early November. Garfield's concerns over the political situation in Indiana were mollified by the middle of the month. His relief can be sensed on October 13: "Our plurality in Indiana will be about 20,000. By noon the magnitude of the victory had increased. By night it was certain that we had carried Indiana by over five thousand, had gained two Congressmen, and probably captured the legislature." The next day he also had Ohio on his mind: "Telegrams and letters from all sides. The effect in Indiana and Ohio has been overwhelming." By October 15, the candidate seemed overwhelmed by his own party's success: "Letters and telegrams of congratulations are pouring in so rapidly that I am compelled to abandon the purpose of answering them except a few of the most important." This proved to be a rare moment in which Garfield did not want to please everybody all of the time. While he may have felt good about the state elections in Indiana, he tempered this enthusiasm with a warning to a campaign member on the fifteenth: "The elections on Tuesday last greatly simplified the conditions of the contest. They have brought fresh and valuable reinforcements to the field, but they have also brought us some of the dangers that always attend success, especially that arising from overconfidence." Garfield then pointed out that the contest would shift to New York. He proved to be right with his predictions.[26]

After the state elections in Indiana and Ohio, the groups descending on Garfield's home became larger, with newspapers such as the *Chicago Tribune*

and the *New York Herald* printing articles about these events. While partisanship dominated most of them in 1880, newspapers focused more on the
personalities of the candidates, rather than the parties they represented, since
that was the best way to sell the most copies. Garfield's efforts fit nicely with
this growing trend. On October 15 the general wrote that "about fifty ladies
from Painesville" came to Lawnfield, soon followed by a "large number of
ladies" brought to the house by a missionary society and accompanied by an
"unusual number of gentlemen." Later that day he wrote that "a thousand
businessmen of Cleveland came on a special train of thirteen cars. Mr. Ely delivered an address to which I replied in a short speech." Apparently, Garfield
was about to address "the largest delegation of the kind that had ever went
out of Cleveland." The general told his listeners that they actually played three
roles in society—businessmen, citizens of Ohio, and citizens of the United
States—and spoke to all three mind-sets. First, he addressed the onlookers as
businessmen, telling them that if they elected him as president, it would be
like taking out a four-year policy guaranteeing their freedom from unnecessary
government interference: "The power that could underwrite such a policy to
you would call from you more sacrifice in a mere business sense than you ever
made under any circumstance." He also reminded the men of their ancestry
as Ohioans. Finally, when Garfield addressed them as Americans, he touched
on a topic close to his heart: "You, as citizens of that Republic [the United
States] have a right to walk on every foot of it as the equal of any man that
lives anywhere, and that the score of black men that I see have just as good
a right as the whitest of us all."[27]

   Garfield seemed aware that he was talking to a group that needed to hear
that, with government deregulation, there must be restraint on their part
so the rights and wages of average workers would be protected. He also
knew that there were African Americans in his audience, so he addressed
them as well. By 1880 southern state governments were under the control
of the Redeemers following the formal end of Reconstruction three years
earlier; African Americans around the country were rightfully nervous about
the future of these and other state governments. Southern Democrats had
continued to attack voting-rights laws that protected black voters into the
spring of 1880, fearing that Republicans were trying to create a biracial coali-
tion with African Americans that would challenge their own perception of
the "natural order of society." One southern Democratic organ claimed, "It
is a struggle for existence, for civilization, for the very hearthstones of the
people. . . . Should this ignorant class, wrought up into a pitch of political

fanaticism," be allowed to elevate "a set of Vandals to the White House?" This type of rhetoric made for happy Republican leaders, who wanted the southern question to be one of the two main issues during the upcoming canvass (along with the tariff schedule). Other Republican campaigners talked about the plight of African Americans, whose rights served as the primary subject in twelve of the nineteen chapters in the Republicans' campaign textbook. In 1866 Garfield looked like a staunch defender of African Americans' Fourteenth Amendment rights when he said of one Ohio Democrat and political opponent regarding black rights on the House floor, "It is not the first time that gentlemen on that side of the House, have asked the South to rally against the North." Yet he had also supported the Compromise of 1877, which ended Reconstruction.[28] African American onlookers and people reading newspaper accounts of this interlude probably saw right through the lip service Garfield was offering up. Here was a candidate telling his African American visitors that he believed in their right to equality and citizenship while as a congressman he saw Reconstruction come to an abrupt end and the slow rise of Jim Crow segregation begin.

In what was becoming an integral part of the front porch campaign, all of the businessmen were invited inside Garfield's home to meet the candidate and his family after his talk. For a half hour, Garfield had something "pleasant to say to nearly every man." A German spoke to the candidate in "the language of the fatherland," and Garfield replied in German. Another man claimed to have fought at the Battle of Chickamauga, to which Garfield responded: "You were there? I am *very* glad to see you." An older man named John A. Foot greeted the candidate, who quipped, "I suppose you are one of the 'First Voters.'" Another older man told him that he had voted for "Old Hickory," Andrew Jackson, twice and planned to do the same for Garfield. The former general also saw a man he had fought with during the Civil War named Gen. J. J. Elwell, joking to him, "When are you going to send me any more dispatches like those sent when I was answering Mill?" This kind of friendly behavior might have turned around some voters' opinion of Garfield, Democrats having started several rumors about him. One partisan paper had claimed that the Republican had stolen furniture from a southern widow during the Civil War, but his affable persona during these campaign visits made him seem unlikely to have stolen a woman's furniture, particularly when he was so readily willing to share access to his own home and furnishings.[29] Garfield knew how to give a speech without offending anyone and at the same time possessed the ability to personally meet different kinds of prospective voters and make them feel comfortable.

Some local sheets gave the candidate's efforts a glowing review. The *Cleveland Herald* claimed that the trip was "more than a success. It was a grand demonstration of the businessmen of Cleveland. It was more than just a demonstration, for it was a jubilee." The report contended that if a straw poll was taken at the gathering, then Republicans would have received 867 votes, while the Democrats, Greenbacks, and undecided columns would have garnered none. The description of the crowd made it sound organized as the visitors marched in lockstep toward Lawnfield. When Garfield made his appearance, "a rousing cheer was sent up—not hollow and wooden, but full of ring and overflowing with meaning." The *Painesville Telegraph* also praised Garfield's efforts and printed reminders for a "Grand Rally at Mentor" on the last day in October. This notice had a large picture of an American flag underneath it and a description of the event that read, "Afternoon street parade and Evening Torch-Light Procession." A further description appeared underneath: "The Lake County Boys in Blue unite with those of Geauga and Ashtabula in a Grand Rally and Parade at Mentor, next Saturday afternoon, and Torch-light Procession in the evening."[30] Based on the sources available, the *Telegraph* was the only newspaper in 1880 to advertise processions to Garfield's house in advance.

There were other newspapers that criticized Garfield for his visits as well as his visitors for their allegedly vulgar behavior. The *Cleveland Plain Dealer,* in an article titled "TAFFY FOR GARFIELD," referred to the businessmen from Cleveland as the "alleged Republican Men's Business Club" and opined that the throng numbered so many because they had been given a "free ride" by train to Lawnfield. Two days later the *Plain Dealer* attacked Garfield for his lack of specificity on the politically important issue of the tariff. The paper contended that the candidate had said some "very neat things" while giving a "rather slushy speech" and in the process had completely avoided the subject, pointing out that he was supposed to be espousing a protective tariff. Finally, it asked its readers what they expected from a member of the Cobden Free Trade Club. A few days later the *Plain Dealer* also attacked a group of men from Indiana who had recently visited Lawnfield. The paper derisively noted that these so-called businessmen did not impress Ohioans as "any great shakes," positing that some of them looked like "large dealers in wet groceries and repeating states." It also contended that if these were the "specimens of the high moral idea party of Indiana," then God had certainly deprived that state.[31]

The *Plain Dealer* spent a good deal of time castigating Garfield for dodging the issue of protective tariffs. One story made him seem like anything but friendly while talking to a reporter about it. A newsman from the National Associated Press asked the candidate if he had a minute to spare for a talk, to which Garfield curtly replied, "I haven't time. What do you want?" The man then asked about his views on the tariff; Garfield responded, "I refuse to talk. I say nothing upon that topic to anybody." He reminded the candidate that Hancock had made a public pronouncement about the issue, so voters expected the Republican contestant to say something about it too. Garfield retorted, "I refuse positively to talk." The reporter finally said, "The Democracy say you are inconsistent—that you lean toward free trade." The general finished off the testy interview by flatly stating, "Excuse me, sir; I am about to meet some friends from Indiana and give them some apples." The *Plain Dealer* in reporting this reminded its readers that it was all that could be extracted from the "great statesmen" about the all-important issue of the election.[32]

Not only did African Americans, businessmen, and women from Cleveland come to Lawnfield, but so did a group of German Americans. On October 18 "seven cars loaded with Germans, came from Cleveland, and Mr. Kaufman, the editor of the German newspaper 'Anzeiger,' delivered an address to the people in their native tongue." The *Indianapolis Journal* estimated that a total of five hundred people made the visit. While the candidate did not speak German fluently, he claimed that he had "caught some of the inspiration of his [Kaufman's] thought, though not all, but enough of it" to respond in English. Garfield admitted to mistakenly referring to a dead German American congressman as a "foreigner," acknowledging that the English people (and by extension their American descendants) drew many of their traditions from Germany, or the "Fatherland," as the general liked to refer to it. He expounded on this by stating that "strong, and yellow haired the blue-eyed Saxons came, they planted the principles of [the] Teutonic in England. . . . [T]he Constitution of Great Britain came from the woods of Germany." Garfield claimed that the United States was better off to have Germans as part of its racial mixture. (He also congratulated the Germans on their recent completion of the Cathedral of Cologne, which had been in the making for 630 years.) Fittingly, he finished his address by reading eight lines (in German) from the poem "Novalis." As the crowd cheered him on, the candidate exclaimed, "Wilkommenialle."[33] Demonstrating a keen knowledge of German history and current events to help him identify with prospective voters, Garfield clearly knew how to play well to his German American audience.

The *Cleveland Herald* argued that this visit signified that the German vote in Ohio would be solidly Republican. Among other things, it noted that the Germans visited almost every part of the farm and were "anxious" to carry away a "memento" from it. Garfield's daughter, who apparently sat in a window of the home with several of her friends watching them milling about the residence, spent an hour tying bouquets for the visitors. The *Herald* pointed out that the bouquets might not last long, but the "sweet face" of the young hostess and her "modest" and "pleasant" ways would not soon be forgotten. Several days later the paper translated the passage from "Novalis" into English: "Come, clasp my hand confiding; Call brother me-abiding, Until death's last dividing, And never before with me. One temple for our praying, One home where we are staying. One joy our hearts is swaying, One heaven for me and thee."[34] Garfield's ability to identify with his foreign-born audience would prove to be important for his presidential aspirations. He won his home state by fewer than 5 percent of the popular vote. With the influx of German immigrants and German-born Americans to Ohio in the nineteenth century, it was vital for Garfield to connect with these voters. It is also important to note that he treated these German laborers in the same personable way that he had treated the businessmen from Cleveland.

Maybe the most fascinatingly dressed visitors to Mentor came on October 19, when 446 members of the Lincoln Club traveled from Indianapolis. The men "wore linen dusters and three cornered straw hats, pinned up in three-cornered Continental style." The straw hats made the Indianans look "comical." Their outfits were designed to caricature the clothing worn by a rival Democratic organization in Indianapolis called the Jefferson Club, whose membership comprised democratic "bloods" sporting "blue flannel suits, white plug hats and white kid gloves." Each visiting member of the Lincoln Club wore two badges. One was a plain, blue, silk badge bearing the inscription "Garfield Lincoln Club, 1880." The other sported a misshaped human head with a large mouth representing the entrance of a "Mammoth Cave": out of the mouth came the words "Telegraph it to the boys"; beneath the head was written "Well, I should smile." This referred to an attempt earlier that year to change the date for Indiana's state elections from October to November; the thinking was that this would help Democratic candidates win. The legislature decided not to make the change. But in between their deliberations and a public announcement, an Indiana Supreme Bench judge named Warden, a Democrat, "rushed" into a Democratic Central Committee meeting and proclaimed to the secretary, "We've done it Jim; telegraph it to the boys."[35] The members of the Lincoln Club were mocking the judge for arrogantly assuming that the changes he wanted made were going to be signed into law so that his party could be more successful.

On their way to Lawnfield, the Indianans marched around the depot singing, "We'll tie Frank Landers to the tale of the mules," which was apparently sung to the tune of "John Brown's Body." Landers was the Democratic Party's candidate for Indiana governor in 1880. Supported by four hundred voices, the song created a "remarkable effect." The men also carried "large brooms" over their shoulders to demonstrate their desire to sweep the Democrats out of office in the fall. When the chant "three cheers for Garfield" was demanded, the combination of voices, straw hats, and brooms were "raised with a vigor that almost shook the depot's walls." As the train rolled along, whenever the men were met with cheers from the side of the tracks, they fired a small cannon from the baggage car, which "boomed terrifically." Interestingly, these loud, aggressive partisans were prominent bankers, merchants, and other businessmen from Indianapolis who could really amp up spectacle-style processions. When the group arrived at Lawnfield, Garfield was "out at a distant point on his farm" because he was not expecting the visit until the next day. Of course, he dropped what he was doing and rushed to the house to meet the men, so that when he arrived "his cheeks glowed like roses in the bracing morning air." When the candidate stepped out onto his front porch to speak, the Indianans "cheered wildly" and were "highly pleased by his appearance."[36]

In his remarks to the group, Garfield clearly appreciated the symbolism of the Lincoln badges and the outfits, noting that "the old three cornered hat" reminded him of the Revolutionary generation. He had heartfelt, historically based compliments for men who were wearing outfits that seemed "comical" to some observers: "Now these representatives of Indiana come representing the Revolution in your hats, representing Abraham Lincoln in your badges and representing the victory both of the Revolution and of Lincoln in the news you bring. I could not be an American and fail to welcome your costumes, your badges, your news and yourselves." The candidate opined that Lincoln's Emancipation Proclamation was a second Declaration of Independence for America. Garfield also recalled an instance near Corinth, Mississippi, during the Civil War when he needed some men to cut some wood. He noted that the 55th Indiana Regiment had "chopped down more trees in a half a day then I supposed it was possible could fall in any forest in a week. It appears that in the great political forest from which you have just come your axes have been busy again." The *New York Herald* thus referred to these visitors as "Axe men."[37]

When Garfield finished addressing the Lincoln Club, "all" had the pleasure of shaking hands with him. In the parlor the men were introduced to Mrs. Garfield and the couple's daughter. The candidate and his twelve-year-old daughter, who was unanimously voted a "favorite" by "all" in the club, signed autographs. The men also walked by the cornfield, the kitchen garden, the flower garden, and the orchard. At noon the club marched down the lane by Garfield's house with banners in hand and gave three cheers "for the next president." The *New York Herald* titled their article about the event "The Republican Mecca." The *Indianapolis Journal* claimed that "a more enthusiastic crowd was never seen at Mentor."[38] This was exactly the type of press coverage that Garfield needed. Amid extreme economic change, voters throughout the United States could read about average people going into a presidential candidate's home, meeting his family, having something to eat, and even picking vegetables from his gardens. The Indianans also embodied the type of spectacle politics that Republicans were famous for. This may have been the most exciting event of the campaign.

On October 20 Garfield made more comments on race when 250–300 African Americans came to Lawnfield from Cleveland. The group toured the farm before seeing the candidate and "carrying off from the lawn, field, farm, as souvenirs of the flowers, apples, turnips and corn that the numerous white delegations proceeding them had left untaken." The leader of the group, J. P. Green, stated: "We have seen swept away from us, one by one, the ballot box, the jury box and the right of representation, those bulwarks of liberty without which perfect liberty is but a barren ideality. . . . Our fathers, brothers, and children have been murdered in cold blood while trying to assert these rights . . . , and today thousands of them are refugees on the bleak plains of the far West in search of homes. General, we feel that we need a strong arm and sympathetic heart enlisted in our cause. . . . [W]e believe that with you in the Presidential chair our desires . . . shall have been realized." Garfield responded: "I have studied your problem with no little solitude. . . . [O]f all the problems that any nation ever confronted none was ever more difficult than that of settling the great race question." He claimed that not only did slavery wrong the black race but also "was dangerous to the peace and prosperity of the white race and to the stability of the Republic." Garfield also admitted, "when you were free[d] by the proclamation of Lincoln and by the amended Constitution that gave you citizenship your problem was not solved." He warned: "Permit no man to praise you because you are black, nor wrong you because you are black. Let it be understood that you are ready and will-ing to work out your own material salvation by your own energy, your own worth, your own labor." The candidate recounted his experiences with a black senator in Washington: "I have seen your representatives in Congress—one in the Senate—and I have seen them behave with such self-restraint, good sense, judgment, modesty, and patriotism that it has given me new hope." Garfield then invited each man to personally meet him, but newspapers did not report the African Americans entering his home.[39]

Some sheets mocked the candidate for his performance. The *Washington Post* headlined the event "WHY SLAVERY CEASED" and underneath it stated, "The Story as Told to a Lot of Negroes at Mentor." The *Cleveland Plain Dealer* referred to Garfield's audience as "coons" and claimed that after his talk, the candidate nudged Patrick Henry and said, "God, save me from my friends." Conversely, the *Cleveland Herald* opined that Garfield's speech was "wholly devoid of demagoguery." It argued that, while Andrew Johnson had promised black folks that he would be their Moses and "lead them to the promised land," Garfield's language had proven to be entirely different. Garfield had provided his audience with some down-to-earth, straight talk, "not a word, not a syllable smacking of clap-trap fell from his lips." The paper praised the candidate for not promising his listeners that he would be their Moses and for the "total absence of gush" from his speech.[40] While Republican leaders were certainly moving away from civil rights for African Americans as an important party plank, black voters still regarded the party as the lesser of two evils when compared to the Democratic Party, which was seeing its southern leadership being taken over by Redeemer governments.

The large groups that descended upon Mentor starting on October 20 un-wittingly performed another important campaign function for Garfield: they provided a distraction for a nation of newspaper readers from the infamous "Morey Letter," which was reprinted that day in journals around the country. In the letter dated January 23, 1880, Garfield had written to H. L. Morey that he supported the use of Chinese workers in US factories and that the owners of production had the right to buy the cheapest labor they could find. Garfield claimed that a treaty with the Chinese preserved the right for American busi-nesses to use their emigrant countrymen's labor and that the treaty should be "religiously kept." Morey died in the fall of 1880, and the letter was found in his effects. Newspapers such as the *Springfield Republican* printed the correspondence on one page and then on the next page delivered positive news about Garfield's speech to his African American visitors from Cleveland. While his opponents tried to detract from the Republican's candidacy by reprinting the damning letter, his visits and speeches from his front porch allowed Garfield to put a positive spin on the daily news cycle covering his campaign. He also denied writing the letter and claimed that it was forged.[41]

On October 21 twelve hundred Civil War veterans came to Lawnfield, traveling by train from Cleveland. They fired off a cannon as they passed through each town on the way. The men were an "imposing spectacle" as they exited the train, marched to Garfield's home in columns of four, and were led by two bands playing music. The *Cleveland Herald* claimed that the group had an "internal affection" for the general that no other group visiting Lawnfield could possibly have. The candidate greeted them and told the men about the first political stump speech that he had ever heard. In the middle of this talk by Joshua R. Giddings, a southerner took out a pistol "in favor of human liberty and marched over toward him to shoot him down." Garfield claimed that Giddings replied, "I knew I was speaking for liberty and I felt that if the assassin shot me down my speech would still go on and triumph." He claimed that the men in front of him now were there in the same spirit that Giddings had been and embodied the spirit that motivated men to fight in the Civil War. Finally, tying them to the larger martial experience, Garfield remarked that after Napoleon had died, some of his soldiers still felt that there were certain "anniversary days" in which their former leader would do midnight inspections of them. He admitted a hope that he shared that kind of a bond with his soldiers. A few days later, a man calling himself "An Old Veteran" wrote a letter to the *Cleveland Herald* assuring Garfield that the "immortal 1,200" would be expecting a review from him every October 21 once they had all arrived in heaven.[42]

Garfield's remarks to his African American and Civil War–veteran visitors did not signify a strong desire in the candidate to "wave the bloody shirt," which many Republican candidates had done in order to effectively court partisan support during the Reconstruction period. In the ensuing Gilded Age, politicians, authors, participants, religious leaders, and various other leaders in communities across America tried to mold the memory of the Civil War to fit their emotional and cultural needs as a society. As David Blight posits, three general schools of thought about the memory of the war started evolving during these years: reconciliatory, white supremacy, and emancipatory.[43]

Reconciliatory thinkers wanted to remember that both sides were right for fighting the war, white supremacists thought the South was justified for defending their right to own slaves, while emancipatory thinkers stressed the role that slavery and freedom played in the war. Garfield's remarks to black and veteran voters communicated that he took an emancipatory view of the memory of the war. He did not talk down to African Americans and note their value as second-class citizens (as a white supremacist would have), nor did he want to reconcile with the old Confederacy; there is no record of any Confederate veterans being welcomed by the candidate at his home. The memory of Garfield's role as a general during the Civil War also helped promote his masculinity, while his appearances from his front porch asserted his domestic sensibilities. Republicans wanted voters to see Garfield as a family man who was sensitive to the needs of his wife and children without attacking his masculinity—his status as a Civil War general and the memory of his wartime deeds helped achieve this delicate balancing act. By maintaining that balance, Republicans were able to unify behind a strong candidate.

A visit from Civil War veterans was more than just symbolic because of Garfield's own participation; their pension benefits proved to be a touchy subject for Republicans and Democrats during the Gilded Age. The issue was directly tied to protection of the home and family for Republicans, which made the veterans' visit even more significant. In 1862 Republicans in Congress had passed a generous pension act, which offered economic protection to wounded soldiers as well as the wives, mothers, and sisters of deceased soldiers. By the end of the war, most of the pension payments were being received by women related to those who died in service. Even as late as 1875, half of these payments went to female-headed households.[44] Direct visits between Garfield's family and veterans reaffirmed the party's commitment to protecting the homes of injured soldiers and the women related to those who died by honoring their pensions. In contrast, Confederate veterans and their spouses received nothing from the federal government.

Following the visit from the veterans, rain curtailed events in Mentor for the next four days. Afterward, on October 26, "600 Trumbull County people" came to Lawnfield from the nearby town of Warren. Garfield's successor in the House of Representatives, judge Lane B. Taylor, introduced the candidate. Garfield thanked the crowd as vociferously as possible and noted that he could see among them many personal friends from over the years; he reminded everyone that no one had better leave his home without shaking his hand. The gendered political roles of the visiting men and women surfaced when the women went inside the Garfield home "to seek the grateful warmth within," while the men stayed outside to shake the candidate's hand. The *Cleveland Herald* pointed out that the group contained many personal friends of Garfield, so it took "proportionally, more time than common" for the candidate to meet all of the men, a process that warranted an "extra pressure."[45]

Garfield received an interesting visit the next day when nine hundred women from Cleveland and the surrounding area came to his home. The *Indianapolis Journal* described it with the headline, "General Garfield's Front Yard Inundated by a Wave of Feminine Loveliness and Patriotism—His Usual Apt Response." While riding the train to Lawnfield, the women waved their handkerchiefs and hats as they were cheered by onlookers. When the candidate appeared, they gave him a "Chautauqua salute" and the obligatory "loud applause." The chairwoman of the group introduced Garfield, who noted the historical significance of this type of meeting: "It seems to me, as I look upon this assemblage, that there could be no such scene as this in any but a free country." He explained that in a monarchy "the governing power does the governing itself," but in the United States "the real governing power in this country never does the actual work of government, but causes it to be done by agents and servants." Garfield complimented the women for their services in the late war, having helped "execute the nation's will." He finished by pointing out that "this unique exhibition of American spirit—this spirit which inspired our soldiers while fighting, succored them in sickness, and consoled them in dying . . . is but another manifestation of the growing power of home upon America." Afterward, he announced that Mrs. Garfield wanted to meet every one of them before they left the household.[46] The candidate artfully managed to dodge the subject of women's suffrage, about which he had received several letters from Susan B. Anthony during the summer of the campaign.[47] Once again Garfield offered up lip service to the attending women, but no substantial promises on future suffrage legislation. Following the shallow talk, the visitors all came into the house and were personally greeted by Garfield, his mother, his wife, and their daughter. The family was given some floral offerings, "consisting of a straw basket containing some beautiful grasses for Grandma Garfield, a large floral horseshoe for General Garfield, a large basket of choice and tastefully arranged flowers for Mrs. Garfield, and an exquisite bouquet for Miss Mollie Garfield." The donor of the flower arrangements preferred to remain anonymous. Some of the women picked apples from the family farm to take home with them as souvenirs, but most refrained in order to show a good example for other groups visiting the farm. One of the attendees, an eighty-three-year-old Mrs. Willer, had at one time kept an "Old Commercial House in Cleveland when Garfield drove a canal horse."[48] The *Cleveland Herald* did not mention whether or not Mrs. Willer had known Garfield when he was a youth.

Politicians in Washington received growing pressure to take women's suffrage on a national level more seriously. Western territories formed at this time often allowed for women's suffrage in their constitutions. Wyoming Territory, for example, gave women the right to vote with its formation in 1869, with the reorganized Utah Territory following suit in 1870. Extending suffrage could potentially help these eventual states claim more representatives in the House as well as Electoral College votes and made voters back east wonder what the future of America's voting laws might look like. Groups such as the American Women's Suffrage Association and the National Women's Suffrage Association had become exasperated with both major parties by 1880 because of their refusal to directly back a national women's suffrage amendment. While women knew that Republicans were more likely to at least support this expansion, suffrage supporters did not think that Garfield was of their ilk, one stating, "while I freely admit that Women Suffrage is not directly an issue in this campaign and that General Garfield is not a Suffragist, I still think it is greatly for the interest of Woman Suffrage that the Republican Party should retain control of the government." In contrast, some New York suffragists, including Lillie Devereux Blake, Susan King, and Clemence Lozier, met with Hancock and decided to support him. They publicly endorsed the Democrat and actively stumped for him in 1880 in New York—a key battleground state in the contest.[49] All of these factors made it even more important for the Republican to put on an effective event and appear empathetic, at least publicly, to the political plight of women.

Despite straddling the issue of women's suffrage, Garfield's use of his wife at his home helped contrast the campaign roles of the candidates' wives and highlighted the party's differing gendered political philosophies. With her at his side, Garfield publicly appeared as a family man. One of his campaign biographers celebrated the Republican as "a devoted husband and father." Another biographer highlighted that Lucretia Garfield loved different cultures and learning in general, and he posited that "much of General Garfield's success in his subsequent career may justly be attributed to his fortunate marriage." Mrs. Garfield did not make speeches from the front porch but did meet voters afterward, invite them into her home, make small talk, and allow folks to leave with gifts from the family farm. In contrast, Hancock and his wife, Almira Russell, never met large groups of voters together at their home or on the road. In Hancock's campaign biographies, his wife was virtually unmentioned and faceless. These biographies contained plenty of military portraits of the general and pictures of a masculine Hancock in Civil War battles but very few pictures of his family. They also celebrated his masculinity and adventurousness: "The boy was by no means a prodigy either of studiousness or learning. He grew to be a rugged, large-boned lad, fond of gymnastic exercise and wild sports."[50] The use, or lack thereof, of the candidates' wives reflected both parties' gendered political philosophy: Republicans were sharers of their homes with their wives, while Democrats dominated their wives in the domestic setting.

The last day of October was the busiest day at Mentor and the apex of the first front porch campaign season. Approximately 2,200 people came through the Lawnfield home that day. First came 150 ironworkers from Youngstown, Ohio, wearing badges on their hats with the number 329 on them and accompanied by a cornet band.[51] When Garfield arrived to see them, he was dressed for the occasion: "In the buttonhole of his coat lapel the General wore a bouquet of yellow and blue pansies." The candidate was clearly prepared for several public appearances throughout the day and ready to advertise himself as the man for the job. Garfield told the ironworkers that if "we were at war with the rest of the world we could by our skill clothe and equip ourselves and make all the tools and machinery for our own use, without drawing on other nations for a single hammer stroke." This was the true significance of their industry to Garfield. He went on to describe their work as "patriotic" before inviting them all to come and shake his hand. After the speech the cornet band played "The Star-Spangled Banner."[52] This was a classic example of spectacle politics.

The ironworkers were followed by "450 strong" citizens from West Salem, Ohio, who were accompanied by a cornet band as well as the West Salem Glee Club. Afterward, while the singers were performing in Garfield's house, a group of one hundred steelworkers from Britton Iron and Steel Works out of Cleveland came through. In his speech to them, the candidate made an interesting reference to European tradition: "It is said that Prince Bismarck, one of the ablest men in Europe, had for his motto, 'Iron and Blood.' That is pretty strong, but we have for our motto, 'Iron, together with all the other industries, and liberty.'"[53] Later that day "about fifteen hundred members of clubs came from all parts of Lake County and from several towns of Ashtabula, Geauga and Cuyahoga" and arrived at Lawnfield. Garfield noted that "shortly after noon it began to rain, and the storm grew in violence into the night. But the clubs, cavalry and foot, paraded in the field south of the road, until after dark."[54] The *New York Times* reported that the "multitudes of people stood in the rain watching the parade. The enthusiasm was not dampened by the weather." According to the *New York Herald,* the groups "displayed numerous transparencies and mottos," including "We'll stand by our old representative," "Down with free trade," "Garfield and Protection," "Prosperity, peace and plenty," and "Ohio wants a change in Congress."[55] While the Republican candidate did not promise any of the groups anything specific on that final day of his campaign, he did invite each of them into his house and made a point to shake each individual's hand.

On November 1, Garfield spent a "quiet" day in Mentor, with no visitors calling on him. The *New York Herald* reported that the candidate was calm and "not worried about the probabilities of the election." Garfield described the day as "a Lull along the whole line of battle." Just as quickly as the first front porch campaign in American history picked up in mid-October, it came to a halt on the first day of November. A few days later Garfield won the contest in what was the closest popular vote in presidential-election history. The night of the election, "75 Republican gentlemen" were with their man at his home, but there is no evidence that the new president-elect addressed them when the results came in. One day after the contest, 379 people visited Mentor. Garfield greeted these guests but did not give a speech to them. The Republican candidate garnered 4,454,416 votes, while Hancock received 4,444,952 votes. More important, Garfield secured 214 electoral votes to Hancock's 155 votes. In New York, Garfield won 555,544 votes, while Hancock received 534,511 votes. In Indiana, Garfield tallied 232,164 ballots to Hancock's 225,522. Finally, in Ohio, Garfield defeated Hancock 375,048 to 340,821.[56]

Garfield's events made both positive and negative impressions on their onlookers. The *Cleveland Plain Dealer* claimed that so many people visited Mentor because they were offered free rides "at somebody's expense" to hear the "linguist of Lawnfield" and then "go for his garden." It described the Young Men's First Voters group raiding the orchard, the Indiana businessmen "catching on to" Garfield's corn, the "radical Germans" basking in his German poetry while gobbling his turnips, and the "coons" collaring the candidate's chickens.[57]

A few days later the *Plain Dealer* produced another scathing indictment of Garfield's style, describing what his conversations with his wife must have been like when the throngs of visitors descended upon Lawnfield. Allegedly, one night at two o'clock in the morning, Mrs. Garfield woke up to "Comanche

yells" coming from the front of her house and asked her husband what he was
going to do. The candidate comforted his wife by stating, "don't be alarmed my
dear, it's another of those Cleveland delegations; I can hear Charlie Babcock's
voice," then crawling "wearily out of bed and poking around the dark for his
pantaloons." Just after Garfield returned to bed, another group showed up,
and Mrs. Garfield "groaned and muttered. . . . There's another batch coming.
I'd know the leader's voice anywhere; it's Ol' Scoville." It also cracked that if
the candidate did not shake the people's hands, then his visitors would insist
on staying for a week. The *Plain Dealer* finished its lampoon of Garfield's plight
by pointing out that the candidate must have deeply regretted building his
house so close to Forrest City as he had most likely promised an appointment
to be a postmaster or a collector to every Republican in the area.[58]

Other visitors to Lawnfield, such as Whitelaw Reid, came away impressed
by the candidate. Reid visited Mentor on September 23: "There was about
him [Garfield] not a trace of self-consciousness of a successful candidate. His
happy spirit appeared to draw nothing of its vitality from the political situation. Sauntering arm in arm with his guests down the lanes of the Mentor
home, his easy, interesting talk was now of the prosperous fields on either
hand, and now of bookish things. The impression he left was of a mind and
personality equally strong, original and lovable." Reid also wrote that "the
more they [voters] learned of his career, his studies, his ideas, and his daily
life, the stronger he became."[59] Garfield appears to have been a self-confident
man who did not come off as arrogant. He was good at making transitions
in conversation from talking about farming subjects to "bookish things," or
intellectual, academic topics.

James Blaine was in chorus with men like Reid in his positive estimations
of Garfield as a candidate. Later, during his eulogy at the assassinated president's funeral, the senator from Maine pointed out: "One aspect of Garfield's
candidacy was unprecedented. Never before in the history of partisan contests
in this country, has a successful candidate spoken freely on passing events
and current issues. To attempt anything of the kind seemed novel, rash, and
even desperate." Blaine went on to note the failures of Greeley and Scott from
the stump but was apparently unaware of Harrison's efforts in 1840. He also
referred to the worries of others regarding public gatherings: "Unmindful of
these warnings, Garfield spoke to large crowds as he journeyed to and from
New York in August, to a great multitude in that city, to delegations and deputations of every kind that called at Mentor during the summer and autumn."
The senator stressed that Garfield never made any mistakes in his talks, for

which his opponents were waiting: "With innumerable critics, watchful and eager to catch a phrase that might be turned into ridicule or odium, or a sentence that might be distorted to his own or the party's injury, Garfield did not halt nor trip in any one of his seventy speeches." Blaine also appreciated Garfield's speaking style, reflecting, "This seems all the more remarkable when it is remembered that he did not write what he said, and yet spoke with such logical consecutiveness of thought and such admirable precision of phrase as to defy the accident of misreport and the malignity of misrepresentation."[60]

Even Democratic leaders praised Garfield for his speeches after the contest. A. F. Rockwell wrote that toward the end of the election, a "distinguished" Democrat noted at a convention of his party that the Republican candidate's impromptu speeches had been a surprising success. This "eminent public man" said, "when Garfield began making speeches to the committees of all kinds calling upon him, I felt sure he would blunder into saying something that would be a dead-weight for him and an advantage for us." Apparently, at least some Democratic leaders were keeping a close eye on Garfield during his front porch campaign. This observer continued: "But watching every word he has said, I am astonished that he has not made a single mistake in all of these talks out of which any capital could be made against him."[61] His front porch performances may have looked simple, but they were not: the trick was to avoid making any public misstatements. Garfield adroitly avoided committing such errors, and the campaign technique certainly caught the attention of Democrats as the race wore on. In addition, no reports of criminal activity or hooliganism in Mentor surfaced over the summer, allowing the first front porch campaign to maintain its bucolic aura.

Despite the criticism from the *Plain Dealer,* October 1880 proved to be an exciting, inventive time in US presidential politics as Garfield's front porch campaign blossomed. The candidate's personality, combined with his family's willingness to participate, his handler's ability to organize, and the design and location of his Lawnfield home, all made it possible. The election saw 9,218,958 voters go to the polls, with Garfield winning by just under 10,000 votes. The front porch campaign, and the newspapers' coverage of the events it produced, may have served as critical components of this narrow victory in the popular vote. While Hancock looked disengaged in the press reports, Garfield spoke to thousands of strangers from his front porch, then he invited them inside his home and shook their hands. The effort helped advertise the Republican brand as personable and family oriented. The rural backdrop that Mentor provided also assisted Garfield in appearing to hold on to Jeffersonian ideals despite the rise of the Hamiltonian vision in increasingly industrialized America. Eventually, Republican sheets in different regions of the country started covering the events, which helped the party start to centralize behind a strong, somewhat charismatic candidate. Finally, the press chronicled many of Garfield's articulate words for, and amicable behavior toward, average people from virtually all walks of life. This type of campaigning must have resonated with voters, not only those who had the opportunity to enter into Garfield's home and meet his family but also the people who read about these interludes in the paper. In the process of meeting the voters face-to-face, Garfield started an effective campaign technique.

CHAPTER 2

Trains, Canes, and Handshakes

Benjamin Harrison's 1888 Front Porch Campaign
for the Presidency

On June 25, 1888, within seconds of hearing the news that Benjamin Harrison had garnered the Republican nomination for the presidency at the party's Chicago convention, journalists reported seeing a "surging throng of excited and yelling men" at the corner of Market and Pennsylvania Streets in Indianapolis. According to accounts in the *Indianapolis Sun,* one ruffian took out a revolver and fired it "rapidly six times" in celebration. With crowds gathering from all directions, a thousand people soon thronged in front of the candidate's downtown office, screaming, "Harrison, Harrison!" Taking Harrison's bow from his office window as a sign, they ran inside and "frantically" reached for his hand.

The citizens who congratulated the new nominee found themselves part of a surprisingly physical encounter. A young man exclaimed, "Here goes my first vote, general!" and the candidate received a handclasp of "unusual warmth." A female employee of Harrison's office reportedly threw her arms around the nominee's neck and kissed him, saying, "Oh, general, I am so glad." Following this interlude, Harrison proceeded to his home on North Delaware Street, where a "small crowd of enthusiasts"—including "many ladies," friends, and acquaintances—awaited his arrival. Asked by one neighbor if she planned to prepare a few cans of fruit to use in the White House, Caroline Harrison, the candidate's wife, responded that "a harder fight was yet to come" and she would wait until the campaign was over before making such preparations.[1] Such intimate, domestic encounters would become a regular part of the Republican's campaign. Within a few hours of being nominated for the presidency, Harrison had already established a routine that would eventually include his greeting more than 300,000 visitors with speeches, handshakes, and a personal welcome to his house. Following in Garfield's footsteps, these personal touches were the cornerstone of what later became known as Harrison's front porch campaign.

Historians have written a great deal about the content of Harrison's speeches in the 1888 campaign. The Republican candidate was an issue-oriented speaker who espoused a high protective-tariff schedule to safeguard American workers. He promoted electoral reform, calling for improved voter-registration laws and district-apportionment rules and speaking out against ballot stuffing. Other issues in the Republican campaign that season included the federal-revenue surplus, Civil War pensions, the Homestead Act, workers' pension benefits, railroad regulation, and civil service support for benevolent and penal associations.[2] Front porch campaigning also made the candidate accessible to the people. Just like the experience with Garfield, workers who barely had contact with their bosses could now shake hands with Harrison, meet his family, and walk on his lawn and front porch. While Indianapolis was bigger than Mentor, it was not a heavily industrialized city, so for many who visited the midwestern "island community," it still preserved small-town, rural ideals despite some recent economic growth. Like Garfield, Harrison and his family received groups that represented a cross section of American society, including businessmen, laborers, women, young voters, children, Civil War veterans, African Americans, and naturalized citizens. On June 26 newspapers reported the positive, personable events to millions of prospective voters around the country, once again unifying Republicans from different regions behind a strong and well-merchandized presidential candidate offering help to average Americans. Unfortunately, like his predecessor, Harrison only offered platitudes and lip service to the minorities and women who came to Indianapolis. He never promised substantial reform measures on race relations, this only a year before the official onset of Jim Crow legislation throughout the South.

Campaign styles in the 1870s and 1880s focused on parades, pageantry, celebration, and alcohol consumption. In the 1880s political organizers transitioned to a more sober, analytical approach, called "educational" campaigning in the Northeast, that emphasized meetings, reading about the issues, hearing from "experts," and discussing problems in an orderly manner.[3] Harrison's front porch campaign combined these two styles. Parades of visitors through Indianapolis on their way to the candidate's home provided the spectacle, then Harrison educated them on the issues from his front porch. Republican newspaper editors also framed the Indianapolis events in a positive way to a national audience, which helped promote the campaign as well organized and smoothly run. Yet balancing elements of hoopla with elements of education was tricky. Despite the troubles the city sometimes faced during the summer of 1888, Republican managers were able to put forth a unified story of campaign organization, excitement, and success through a highly organized press for a national audience to read and feel good about. In an election that saw Harrison win the Electoral College despite losing the popular vote, merchandizing the allegedly impersonal candidate as a friendly neighbor in an average, friendly town proved to be integral to the tight victory.

Harrison's career as a lawyer and politician helped him hone his public-speaking abilities so that he had become an excellent extemporaneous orator by the 1880s. The candidate's great-grandfather had signed the Declaration of Independence, while his grandfather, the successful Whig presidential candidate William Henry Harrison, went on the first presidential speaking tour in 1840. The Republican candidate was born in his grandfather's mansion in North Bend, Ohio, in 1833. His father was a farmer who served two terms in Congress in the 1850s. Harrison was raised a devout Presbyterian and remained active in his faith throughout his life. He attended Miami University in Oxford, Ohio, where he studied the nation's economic laws and worked on his oratorical skills.[4]

In 1853 Harrison married Caroline Scott. The next year he passed the bar, and the couple moved to Indianapolis. They would reside there, or in Washington, DC, for the rest of their lives. The *Springfield Republican* said of Mrs. Harrison, "She is a pure blonde, and when in Washington was considered one of the most beautiful girls, if not indeed, the most beautiful girl in the Senatorial circle." Harrison was a "self-made man" who worked his way up in the law profession and built up a small fortune. About his family name he once said, "Fame is truly honorable and fortune only desirable when they have been *earned.*" In 1857 Harrison joined the new Republican Party and won his first political contest to become the city attorney for Indianapolis. He went on to become the reporter for the state supreme court in 1860 before joining the Union army as a lieutenant in the 70th Indiana Volunteer Infantry. By the end of the Civil War, he had risen to the rank of brevet brigadier general.[5]

In the late 1860s and early 1870s, Harrison moved to the top of the Indiana bar and frequently stumped for Republican candidates for local and state offices. In his professional capacity he helped prosecute lawbreakers associated with the 1877 railway strike. His actions also cemented Harrison's public reputation for having little sympathy for the common man. The Ohio native often came off as socially icy because he did not feel particularly comfortable mingling with people outside of his inner circle of friends and associates. One newspaper wrote that "he does not mingle with the good fellows of the town and slap people on the back, as Garfield had the habit of doing and as Blaine does." Friends and neighbors explained that Harrison was a nice man but walked "with [an] erect military attitude which so many mistake for aristocratic bearing." Nevertheless, in 1880 Harrison was appointed to the US Senate by the Republican-dominated Indiana legislature. During his six years working in that body, he lobbied for Civil War soldier pension benefits and federal aid to education and labored for the admission of Dakota to the Union. He lost the seat in 1887, in part because of legislative reapportionment that once again favored Democrats in Indiana.[6]

As the Republican convention convened at Chicago in June 1888, many insiders considered Senator Blaine from Maine to be the favorite for the presidential nomination. Party leaders adopted a strong protectionist stance, promised to use the federal surplus for veteran's benefits and internal improvements, and insisted on the right of all citizens to vote and have their votes counted. The convention adopted the platform based on these positions unanimously. Although delegates agreed on the issues, they were divided over a nominee. During the course of several days, the convention took a total of eight votes before finally deciding on Harrison as their candidate on June 25, with Levi Morton as his running mate.[7] Now the party had to figure out how to effectively run its ticket against an incumbent president, Democrat Grover Cleveland.

Four years after Garfield's efforts, Blaine had decided to go on a speaking tour as part of his campaign for the presidency. The results were disastrous. First, he was caught eating a private dinner with several millionaires to discuss campaign funding at a fancy restaurant named Delmonico's in New York City; the Democratic press dubbed the dinner "Belshazzar's feast." Then, one week before the election, the candidate was being introduced by the Reverend Samuel D. Burchard, who denounced the opposing Democrats for standing for nothing but "Rum, Romanism, and Rebellion."[8] Party insiders thought that

Blaine's failure to address the slur in part cost him the election because he lost the votes of thousands of Irish Catholics for not defending their honor. Republican campaigners were nervous that another firebrand, Robert Ingersoll, might affect Harrison the same way. A candidate actively campaigning from the stump for the presidency had resulted in only one victory: William Henry Harrison in 1840. Since then, five candidates had toured and lost. But Garfield's front porch campaign had been successful in 1880. On active campaigning, Harrison had previously noted, "There is great risk of meeting a fool at home, but the candidate who travels cannot avoid him." Now he had to decide whether to follow in his grandfather's footsteps, attempt Garfield's approach, or be like his opponent, President Cleveland, who decided to follow a maxim the Founding Fathers would have espoused—the office sought the man, not the other way around. Harrison chose to copy Garfield and allow folks to visit his home. As Charles Calhoun has written, "in the midst of the most important campaign of his life, it seemed a profound waste for him to sit in his parlor and leave the work to others."9

Harrison's campaign managers felt that the family home on North Delaware Street would work well as the backdrop for their effort. *Harper's Weekly* described it as "a plain brick structure, shaded by trees and embellished on one side by a growth of ivy." The house was not "pretentious" but instead "comfortable and reasonably commodious." Harrison was "a good, thoroughgoing Indianapolis citizen. He has the respect of his neighbors, and the love and confidence of every child within walking distance of his own house." A picture of his grandfather, William Henry, was prominently displayed inside the parlor directly above the mantel, and another hung in the hallway. The *Indianapolis Sun* explained that the beauty of the home could be attributed to Mrs. Harrison: "The home owes a large part of its tasteful adornment to her skillful hands, and while not luxurious, it still has the contented air of moderate elegance. There is something peculiarly grateful in the hospitality dispensed in the Harrison home." The *Saint Louis Dispatch* estimated that Harrison's house was worth $20,000 and speculated that it would not rent for more than $800 per month in Saint Louis. Newspaper reporters photographed and sketched rooms in the home that would "take" in their sheets. Harrison's preferred armchair in his study proved to be a particularly popular picture. The *Indianapolis Sentinel* sketched the candidate's study and parlor as well as the first house the couple had lived in when they moved to Indianapolis. Harrison's neighbor across the street, W. H. H. Miller, also had his house lit up "from top to bottom." His other neighbors' homes also looked "conspicuous" as their parlors and lawns were lit up "with the brightness of the day." Allegedly, Harrison had even paid the contractor for building his house in advance, but the man had disappeared from the city with the workers' money before the structure was finished. Once the project was done, Harrison paid all seventeen of the workers "full the stipulated wages" out of his own pocket. Several locals who had helped in the construction publicly backed the story.[10]

As the crowds that gathered at Harrison's home continued to grow in size through the summer, campaign planners elected to move some of his speeches to nearby University Park, between New York and Vermont Streets at what is now the Southern War Memorial. The *Indianapolis Journal* described the venue as being more comfortable for larger audiences than the house. A stand for the candidate had been built on the east side of the park, "handsomely decorated" with flags and protected from the sun by overhanging trees. The view of the speaker was good from all over the park. The paper declared that the number of banners that could be seen on and over the stage made it look "attractive and somewhat profusely decorated." By September, Harrison's handlers had to set up a new, larger platform in the park for their candidate.[11]

With its central location and easy rail access, Indianapolis proved to be a great location for an ever-expanding front porch campaign. *Harper's Weekly* explained that "piety was an inheritance generations strong" for the residents due to a considerable number of New Englanders having helped settle the town in 1780. Men from Indianapolis had fought with William Henry Harrison at the Battle of Tippecanoe in 1811 and had driven local Native Americans off the surrounding lands, which led to the city's growth. Unfortunately, many citizens had suffered greatly from the Panic of 1873, "when the unexpected collapse of the land boom mowed down Indianapolis fortunes like grass in a field." According to *Harper's Weekly,* "only two or possibly three men in the entire city escaped." Although ten of its sixteen banks failed because of the panic, the other six had slowly helped rebuild the local economy. There were now twelve banks in the city, six national and six private. *Harper's Weekly* posited that by 1888, the citizens were "persons of some means, yet few of them are actually rich. Millionaires are as yet painfully scarce in Indianapolis." Despite the financial collapse, the hearty folks of the Indiana capital had pulled themselves up by their bootstraps in the 1870s and 1880s, living up to their ancestors' spirits of piety, toughness, energy, and resiliency. At the end of 1882, the secretary of the Board of Trade reported that 772 manufacturing establishments existed in the city, representing $12,270,000 of its capital, employing about 12,000 people, and producing $30,100,000 of merchantable goods.[12]

The city's growing economy was accompanied by a zeal for politics. On the night of the presidential election of 1884, a man telegraphed a friend in Indianapolis that they were having trouble counting the returns in Detroit, exclaiming, "I wish you'd stop that yelling down there—we can't hear the returns!" The Panic of 1873 and its subsequent economic fallout had seemingly done nothing to quell the political enthusiasm of residents and may have even contributed to their unusual zeal for elections. Indianapolis residents were energetic in organizing their neighborhoods, having formed ninety-four building associations with most working at full capacity. The city also had the second-largest railway center in the country behind Chicago. More than twelve railroads entered the city on their own tracks and were connected to numerous others before entering the new Union Station, having cost $500,000 to build, which was "one of the handsomest and most convenient stations" and, architecturally speaking, "by far the best building in Indianapolis." Located in the center of Indiana, Indianapolis was equidistant from Michigan, Ohio, Kentucky, and Illinois; it was also within "easy speaking distance" of West Virginia. Residents liked to boast that "Indianapolis is the largest wholly inland city in the United States." In elucidating the political significance of Indianapolis, one Democratic leader posited, "As goes Center Township so goes Marion County; as goes Marion County so goes Indiana, and as goes Indiana so goes the Union." Along with Harrison's front porch campaign, Indianapolis also hosted the Indiana State Fair in September 1888.[13]

Harrison's managers operated his campaign with national and state committees as well as an organized group of local supporters. Pennsylvania senator Matthew Quay headed the Republican National Committee out of New York. He was also the chairman of the executive committee, which made him directly responsible for running the presidential campaign. Senator Sherman of Ohio let Harrison know that Quay was the right choice, describing him as "a shrewd, able, and skillful political manager—and has a wonderful facility in gaining the good will of those with whom he comes into contact. Better than this he is an honorable man. He will be true to his promise without evasion or reserve." Quay had been a Republican since the inception of the party in the mid-1850s and had worked tirelessly to make Pennsylvania a Republican state. Throughout the campaign, Quay showed his skill for political management by arranging speeches and other campaign events, financing campaign newspapers, and printing pro-Harrison literature. He also placed national-party funds in the hands of important state operatives to help propel the grassroots aspect of Harrison's campaign. Quay represented "the politics of the old school" because he stressed the power of organization. The senator initially opposed Harrison's efforts from the front porch—in discussing the matter with some friends, he allegedly yelled out, "Shut up General Harrison"—but later in the campaign wired the candidate, "Keep at it, you're making votes." In August, Quay wrote to another campaign advisor, "If Harrison has the strength to do that [keep talking], we could safely close these headquarters and he would elect himself." Harrison also appreciated Quay's contributions to the campaign as it wore on. When the candidate arrived back home from traveling in early September, he wrote to Quay: "The delegations begin tomorrow with me and I shall be put upon trial again in my responses, but I hope to avoid all points of danger. . . . I am very sure that you are managing your end of the campaign well and my ambition will be not to put any stumbling blocks in your way."[14]

Quay not only started changing his mind about Harrison's campaign style but also evolved over the issue of fund-raising. He secured some financing privately but realized that the most effective way to bring in donations was to create a special advisory committee composed of businessmen who already had their colleagues' trust in order to generate the funds. The national committee asked John Wanamaker, a successful Philadelphia department store owner and nationally respected business magnate, to head the committee. Unbeknownst to Quay, Harrison had promised Wanamaker a spot in his cabinet if he assisted in the campaign, so he zealously joined. The Philadelphia entrepreneur also had help from accomplished meatpacker Herman Armour and wealthy industrialist Thomas Dolan. The advisory committee of business experts raised $700,000 and deposited it with the national committee. The impressive sum made up over half of the $1,200,000 that the national committee totaled. Harrison's national organizer, James Clarkson, characterized the special advisory committee's efforts as "sagacious & splendid work in organizing ways & means."[15] The money proved to be vital in fueling the campaign's ability to merchandize its candidate across the country.

While Quay generally supported "the politics of the old school," Clarkson espoused a new style of politicking for votes: educational politics. Michael McGerr has credited him for changing the Republican campaign style from "spectacle" to "educational." Clarkson wanted voters to come to Indianapolis to be educated on the issues by the candidate. A longtime member of the Republican National Committee and Iowa newspaper editor and business-man, Clarkson fought hard for the nomination of Iowa senator William Boyd Allison early in the nominating season. He supported the senator through his newspaper, the *Iowa State Register,* and served as a delegate-at-large for Allison at the statewide meeting of Republicans in Des Moines in March 1888. But despite his best efforts, Clarkson could not gain momentum for Allison outside of Iowa. Later in the campaign season, he argued that the vast majority of Republicans wanted Senator Blaine to garner the nomination.[16] Finally, at the national convention he threw Iowa's support to Harrison. As vice chairman of the national committee, Clarkson coordinated the activities in Indianapolis from an office in New York City with the help of Indianapolis operatives.

Locally, Harrison's campaign quickly created a committee on arrangements to deal with large delegations of visitors and to schedule their proposed visits. On August 17 it announced the formation of the Harrison Marching Society.[17] Members of the society's entertainment subcommittee and a marching band greeted each delegation at Union Station and led the procession, either to the front porch on Delaware Street or to University Park, depending on the size of the crowd. Because the leaders of visiting groups often addressed the crowd before Harrison gave his welcoming address, the local committee inspected the text of every speech for inflammatory or embarrassing remarks. The edited version, given back to the visiting chairman, was reexamined one more time before the person spoke to make "assurance doubly sure" that it fit the campaign's agenda. One Associated Press reporter noted that the candidate also looked over the reports of his talks before they were put out, while two of his associates added that Harrison never made any consequential changes to any texts he reviewed.[18] Following the speeches, most likely the subcommittee for entertainment helped the visitors back to the train station. Harrison and his handlers were clearly aware that effective, disciplined messaging through a national press would help unify the party and properly merchandize his candidacy.

On July 2 the Roman Catholic bishop of Indianapolis, Francis Silas Chatard, visited the Harrison home to meet the candidate and his family. His feelings about the visit echoed Cordyn Fuller's account of a trip to Garfield's Lawnfield residence: "I found him [Harrison] walking on the lawn [674 N. Delaware St.] with his little grandson in his arms. He received me cordially and made the servant conduct me into the house, while he said a few words to some ladies and relatives who were at the gate. Almost immediately he came in and expressed in a cordial manner his appreciation of my visit, and repeated it."[19] These types of interactions put out the perfect vibe for the campaign in conversations among community members about the new "Republican Mecca."

While friendly individual visits were nice, groups that consisted of working-class voters, women, and rural farmers were particularly important to Republicans. The protective-tariff schedule was the major issue between the two parties going into the contest, and Democrats had vigorously tried to convince those groups that they were being hurt by protection. On December 6, 1887, Cleveland attacked the tariff schedule in a blistering message to Congress that generated a tremendous amount of coverage in the press. In the summer of 1888, the House passed the Mills Act, but the Senate blocked the bill; potential reductions on wool duties particularly troubled midwesterners. These moves made the tariff the hallmark issue of the upcoming presidential canvass. Additionally, the Republicans' espousal for a high tariff to protect Americans' jobs, families, and homes fit nicely with their reputation as the "party of the home" and Harrison's front porch style. The candidate, with his wife and children by his side, could promise groups that were hurt by the protective rates that he wanted to shield them too. Harrison also received numerous gifts from his visitors, and many came freighted with symbolic meaning. In one instance the candidate was presented with a "gaudy" umbrella—a symbol of protection—and was told that, while the gift could have been bought twenty-one cents cheaper under no trade restrictions, "if that umbrella had been made without protection wages would have been so low we fellows couldn't have spared time to come over and see you."[20]

The second front porch campaign was full of pageantry as groups from around the country gleefully visited Indianapolis. Each one seemed to try to outdo its predecessor's attempts at creating a spectacle, with banners, fancy gifts for the candidate and his family, costumes, musical bands, and various noise devices. The frenzy created excellent events for Republicans to merchandize. In early July a group of five women from Indianapolis's east side chopped down a seventy-five-foot tree and brought it into town, where they attached flags and streamers to the trunk. The Indianapolis Journal claimed, "The loyal work of these ladies is in the interest of Harrison and Morton and protection to American industries." According to the Journal, "When ladies will drive out into the country . . . , cut down a tree, trim it of its branches, hitch a horse to the trunk and drag it to the road, then chain it to a wagon and drive it to the city; take their shovels and sink the hole in which to raise the pole," then there could be no better show of support for a candidate.[21] The paper rationalized that when a group of women were willing to do such manly, grimy tasks, there could be no more visceral show of support.

Harrison worked hard to link his protective tariff stance to women's issues. On September 15 three hundred members of the Irish-American Republican Club descended on Indianapolis. The group waved a gigantic silk banner that read, "Protection: It's Irish You Know." The banner was presented to the group by young ladies in the capital who were members of the High School Republican Club.[22] Harrison buttressed his stance on a high protective tariff with an analysis of Irish history:

> Who, if not Irish-Americans versed in the sad story of the commercial ruin of the island they love, should be instructed in the benefit influence of a protective tariff? [Continuous cheering.] Who, if not Irish-Americans should be able to appreciate the friendly influences of the protective system upon their individual and upon their home life? Which of you has not realized that not the lot of man only, but the lot of women, has been made softer and easier under its influence? [Applause and "Hear! Hear!"] Contrast the American mother and wife, burdened only with the cares of motherhood and of the household, with the condition of women in many of the countries of the Old World, where she is loaded also with the drudgery of toil in the field.[23]

As Mark Summers has noted, speaking to male voters as members of a family rather than a republic was in vogue by the 1880s.[24] These types of speeches and activities were symbolically important for Harrison because of his espousal for a high tariff. If he really wanted to show his sincerity for protecting American businesses, families, and homes, then what better way to do it than by having women participate in the campaign and speak directly about their role in the family?

Women remained central to the public image of Harrison's front porch campaign. On August 17 two groups from Johnson County, Indiana, and Jacksonville, Illinois, put on a "pretentious" display upon their arrival to Indianapolis. According to the *Chicago Tribune*, "by far the most attractive feature was a glee club of twenty pretty young women, who led the Jacksonville column. They were bewitchingly uniformed in navy blue dresses with encircling broad gold band, light felt men's hats, and carried natty black walking sticks." Entering University Park, the women occupied "a place of honor" in a semicircle facing the speaker's stand. Later that day, "twenty pretty Illinois girls acted as an Amazonian guard to the General and prevented the crowd surging sideways against the moving column." While the campaign stressed that Harrison would provide economic protection for women, sometimes it was the women who had to provide physical protection for Harrison. Summers has argued: "Until the 1880s, women had been, by and large, ornamental more than useful. . . . Now, under the pressure of closely contested elections, the activism mostly found in the Midwest had gone national."[25] Such active demonstrations of female enthusiasm for Harrison, printed in newspapers across the country, projected to women that they were more than just ornaments on the campaign trail and instead were real participants.

Caroline Harrison also played an instrumental role in campaign publicity. What better way to humanize a male political candidate in the newspapers than to describe groups of women coming to visit his wife in their home. One sheet described her as "a typical American woman, strong in her individuality, hospitality, charitable, kindly in manner, attractive in person and forward in all good works." Mrs. Harrison's warmth also helped offset the perception that her husband could be aloof; as one sheet put it: "She is demonstrative, warm hearted, and responsive to the degree of magnetism. Mrs. Harrison is the opposite of her husband, who is quite reserved and often called cold." On October 28 a group of women who formed the Carrie Harrison Club at the ladies' college in Oxford, Ohio, came to meet the namesake of their organization. The president of the group, Mrs. Rachel Martin, stated that each member had already secured pledges for at least one to three votes each for the Republican candidate. Numbering fifty-two young women, thirty-six of whom carried flags, the group led a procession of over fifteen hundred followers to see Harrison. One newspaper commented that "it was a rare sight to witness nearly a hundred uniformed ladies with a female band of sixteen pieces, and marching at the head of a column of nearly fifteen hundred men." The *Indianapolis Sun* reported: "It was a jolly, laughing, happy crowd that Mrs. Harrison greeted, beaming with pleasure. They all enjoyed their visit intensely."[26]

The focus on Mrs. Harrison was particularly important for Republicans. In June 1886 President Cleveland had married Frances Folsom, who proved to be extremely popular in the press and throughout the United States. One pro-Republican newspaper even declared that "no American wedding has attracted such general and such amiable attention." Before running for president, Cleveland had fathered an illegitimate child while living in Buffalo, New York, and had sent money for the boy to his mother, Maria Halpin. The child eventually wound up in an orphanage, in part because Halpin suffered from mental breakdowns and alcoholism. The Democrat suffered for this series of events during the scurrilous campaign of 1884. By marrying, Cleveland had transformed himself in the press into a "respectable family man." The marriage also gave the country a first lady for the first time since the assassination of President Garfield in 1881. Rebecca Edwards has posited that the marriage was Cleveland's most popular act during his first term as president. Within ten weeks of their nuptials, a book titled *The Bride of the White House* told the detailed story of Folsom's life. The text reappeared verbatim in 1888. A new history of first ladies also hit the shelves in time for the election and portrayed Folsom as an excellent first lady: "Her popularity makes her the most potent factor in the administration which the Republicans have to face and fight against." This made Caroline Harrison all the more important. She helped Republicans maintain the aura of being the party of "home life" and proper domesticity in what Edwards has coined "a decade long bipartisan celebration of domesticity," starting with the Folsom/Cleveland marriage.[27] Republican strategists found that Harrison's marriage and proper domestic etiquette served as effective merchandizing angles for their own candidate. Yet while the marketing was effective, Harrison continued his lip service campaign and avoided the issue of female suffrage during his talks to women.

Republicans also used the issue of Cleveland's vetoes of disabled Union soldiers' pension bills as another way to frame themselves as protectors of home life. Since the war, the US Pension Bureau had issued pensions to disabled Union veterans. If the bureau rejected a claim, then Congress usually passed a special pension bill that Republican presidents signed without hesitation. But Cleveland vetoed hundreds of the bills, sometimes mocking their legitimacy. In 1887 Congress tried to pass a dependents pension bill to broaden benefit possibilities for Union veterans, which the president also vetoed. Republicans seized the opportunity to promise disabled veterans a pension if they needed it to protect themselves, their families, or their homes. Union veterans were invited to Harrison's home to buttress the point. In one instance the candidate spoke to a group of two hundred Union prisoners of war, one of whom had both of his feet amputated while in Libby Prison to prevent the spread of gangrene. Harrison told them: "The annals of the war fail to furnish a sadder story than that of the host of Union veterans who suffered war's greatest hardship—captivity. . . . It is the black spot without any lining of silver or any touch of human nature." Here was the former general speaking to men who had been taken from their families for years. The candidate fielded visits from several Civil War groups. In reference to the pension issue, he told one group, "it is not necessary to use the apothecary scale to determine what shall be due those who fought the battles of his country." The next day several Morgan County participants confirmed that Harrison's apothecary-scale comment referenced "the veto machine now at work in the White House."[28] Harrison's statement also publicly reaffirmed his attitude that it was his responsibility to protect Union veterans, and by extension their homes and families, by honoring their deserved pensions.

Besides pension plans, Cleveland also upset the national committee of the Grand Army of the Republic (GAR) in 1887, when he ordered that all confiscated Confederate battle flags stored in the War Department be sent back south. By the late 1880s, some members of the GAR were willing to reconcile with ex-Confederates on some emotional levels, but they were not ready to return their battle flags. Reconciliation did not take away Union veterans' dignity and masculinity, but giving back the southern battle flags seemed to. One member of the GAR stated, "We seem to be sinking into the slum of namby-pambyism and practicing self-emasculation." While they publicly maintained respect for ex-Confederate soldiers, the national GAR organization did not like the Cleveland administration's idea since it took away from all Civil War soldiers' manhood "by displays of sloppy and gushing sentimentality. . . . [T]he men who fought us are full-grown, common-sense men, who look at things in a manly way. . . . Their [southerners] self-respect and consistency are best maintained when we maintain our own consistency and self-respect." As Nina Silber has pointed out, reconciliation politics usually involved celebrating the dignity and masculinity of ex-Confederate soldiers, yet with this statement the GAR maintained respect for them and simultaneously asserted the manhood, pride, and dignity of Union veterans. The Cleveland plan was not enacted. But a year later, when Harrison received a "tattered old battle-flag" from seven survivors of the 21st Illinois Infantry—Grant's original regiment at the beginning of the war—it came freighted with a little extra meaning following the brouhaha over the opposing side's flags.[29]

While Union pensions and Confederate battle flags were on some voters' minds, the Union veterans' trips to Indianapolis also helped them express themselves honestly and proudly. Sectional reconciliation was in its infancy in 1880, when Garfield met members of the GAR in Mentor. In 1885 generals from both sides had participated in Ulysses Grant's funeral—a major sign of reconciliation as legendary Union and Confederate leaders equally participated in the event and publicly shook hands. Surviving soldiers from both sides camped together at Gettysburg in 1887 for the twenty-fourth anniversary of the battle. In July 1888 a member of the Abraham Lincoln Post of the GAR released a list of twenty-four reunions of old Civil War soldiers between 1881 and 1887. People who supported these reconciliatory measures thought that they promoted better business relations and demonstrated a shared "faith" among the veterans. But for many members of the GAR, these reunions made them uncomfortable—they had won the war with pride and in a manly way, yet now they were shaking hands with the losers and marching with them in maudlin ceremonies. It proved to be an emasculating experience to some. As Silber has noted, GAR members frequently blamed reconcilia- tory politicians for making them give up their dignity to the "orchestrated sentimentalism of the reunion culture."[30] The veterans' visits to Harrison's home meant more to the old soldiers than newspapers could capture. These marches in Indianapolis helped restore their own pride in their victory as they represented the Union; they excluded former Confederate soldiers. The veterans' public display of unity during the processions also helped restore their dignity and validated their masculinity as they went to see a former Union general running for the presidency.

In a contest that most experts agreed would be very close, it also became important for both parties to reach out to an entirely different group—young first-time voters. Many older men already knew who they were going to sup- port, which put an even higher premium on securing the allegiance of new voters. This was important for Republicans because Democrats had been concentrating on wooing younger men by talking about issues that would affect them in the future, such as the tariff, and not those related to Civil War pensions or the past. In 1888 both parties established permanent political clubs for young men and held highly publicized national conventions. While most young men's clubs focused on educational politics, several (including organizations for women) visited Indianapolis for some spectacle politics as well. In early August sixty men of the Young Voters' Club from Crawfordsville, Indiana, approached Harrison's home holding "federal" umbrellas. Later that month a group "composed of boys" and "an organization of young voters" came to the candidate's home. In parts of Indiana, Democrats admitted that some of their prospective young supporters had switched political allegiances because of the influence of Carrie Harrison clubs; Republicans also admitted that they had lost some potential followers to Frankie Cleveland clubs. In an illuminating story about the proliferation of youth participation, early in the campaign the *Indianapolis Sun* reported their amusement at seeing "young sweethearts" encounter each other on the streets and express their surprise at the others' penchant for hoopla politics. Neither party could believe that "the other would be guilty of parading the streets, blowing a tin horn or

decorating him or herself like a barberpole and howling like [a] lunatic."
One report had a young couple meeting unexpectedly during one procession:
"'Why George! How you do look!' and 'Well, I do declare, Mary; you down
here, and blowing [a] horn too!'" The paper dramatically declared, "But it
was true those sweet lips were making tin vibrate, and that lovely girl was
pulling and shooting her way through the crowd just as if it were the most
customary thing in the world." The couple then locked arms and started
blowing their horns together as they marched through the crowd.[31]

Children were also instrumental in Harrison's campaign strategy. On
October 8 a group of one hundred women and children, ages ranging from
seven to fifteen years old, came to see him. Six-year-old Charles Pettijohn
headed the group astride a pony, followed by a drum corps of eight boys.
Girls dressed in red, white, and blue carried "mounted Japanese lanterns"
and sang "Marching through Georgia" on their way to the candidate's home,
where they presented the general a "handsome bouquet" of flowers. Harrison told the group: "Children have always been attractive to me. I have
not only entertainment but instruction in their companionship. Little ones
often say wise things. . . . Some of the best friends I have are under ten years
of age, and after to-night I am sure I shall many more, for all your names
will be added." In another instance the Republican encountered a group of
thirty children between the ages of four and twelve on his way home. The
youngsters were all dressed in red, white, and blue and formed a military
procession line on the sidewalk as Harrison approached them. The leader
of the group yelled out to him, "I take great pleasure in introducing to you
these children whose parents are working men and women, and who desire
the success of the Republican Party, the true friend of working men, women,
and children everywhere." The children chanted: "We are for Harrison, he
is the man. If we can't vote, our daddies can." Harrison addressed them and
shook the hand of each "little midget," speaking to several of them personally
in a "fatherly way." This type of publicity was perfect for a candidate who
supported high tariffs to protect families, homes, and the younger members
of American society. In addition, as Summers has posited: "Partisanship . . .
in 1888 . . . was in decline. The parties were not able to wait for members
to come, as in the old days. Especially among the young, the clubs had to
go recruiting."[32] Harrison's willingness to personally meet with children not
only helped him mold a more personable persona among the electorate but
also helped Republicans recruit prospective future supporters in an era of
declining party loyalty. Through his talks with children, Harrison showed

that Republicans were also looking toward the future of politics and not just concerned with problems related to the Civil War.

Like women and children, African American delegations constituted an important additional element to Harrison's front porch campaign. On August 3 "perhaps the most imposing demonstration yet made by citizens from outside the city" came to Indianapolis from Clinton and Montgomery Counties, Ohio. Among the nearly three thousand visitors, the Lew Wallace Club contained some forty "colored" men. Two weeks later a loud group from Rush County arrived in town with forty "colored" men in the line of procession wearing black plug hats. Just two days afterward a group of 150 "colored" Masons, members of the Concordia Commandery on their way to Louisville to attend a Knights Templar convocation, visited Harrison, who with his wife met them at the door of their home. On another occasion several weeks later, the Harrisons even invited some African American visitors into their home for a discussion.[33] Sometimes the candidate talked directly to these African American delegations about their plights in America. To a group of three hundred black members of the Harrison League of Indianapolis, he remarked:

> My memory goes back to a time when colored witnesses were first allowed to appear in court in this State to testify in cases where white men were parties. Prior to that time, as you know, you had been excluded from the right to tell in court, under oath, your side of the story. . . . I have lived to see this unfriendly legislation removed from our statute-books and the unfriendly section of our State Constitution repealed. I have lived not only to see that, but to see the race emancipated and slavery extinct. [Cries of "Amen to that!"][34]

Republican newspapers made sure to add "[Cries of 'Amen to that!']" because the emotion increased their ability to market the event to African American voters reading about it. Republican handlers were determined to brand their presidential candidate as a person who supported black voters. But Harrison refused to directly address the fledgling Jim Crow movement that was already proliferating throughout the South and would result in the codification of such laws by many state legislatures in the coming years.

On September 22 five hundred Republican members of the Chicago Commercial Travelers' Association came to town, embodying spectacle politics maybe more than any other group during the campaign. They were greeted by what one Harrison biographer described as the "entire business community" of Indianapolis. The visitors' march from Union Station to the candidate's house was the grandest procession of a summer filled with such events. An "inspiring scene" unfolded as the jovial group marched down the streets of the capital and great crowds of men and women cheered for them with "lusty voices." Large portraits of Harrison and US flags adorned every building, to which the group waved their flags and their Harrison and Morton banners in reply as they passed. The *Chicago Tribune* reported that "a sea of gaudy sunshades danced to the cadences of the music or kept time with the outbursts of applause." As the police tried to clear out space in front of Harrison's house, the *Tribune* noted that local women were "especially entertained" by the incoming crowd, whose participants waved hats, canes, flags, and "every other movable article." Some of the visitors had unique cases bearing the inscription "Orders from the house, vote for General Harrison," while others handed out cards reading, "A handkerchief, a voice, a pale one dollar; but four slugs of whiskey sour make a howling Democrat." According to the *Tribune,* the folks in Indianapolis all agreed that this was the "jolliest" delegation they had seen yet. Such newspaper reports, which emphasized wide participation and the crowd's excitement, enhanced the success of such "hoopla" politics as well as the campaign's ability to project exciting events to a national audience. Media accounts abetted the Harrison campaign's desire "to draw out the rank and file, both to ratify the nomination by their presence at public events and to stir up a sense of connection with the candidate and the party."[35]

Early in the campaign, Harrison suffered from rumors that he did not care about workers. Later in the contest, rumors also circulated that he was a bigot. Republican strategists chose October 25 as the day to invite more than ten thousand laborers from all parts of Indiana to Indianapolis to give the candidate a public forum to deny the charges. William McKinley was also onstage for the event. An Irish union leader named L. W. McDaniels gave Harrison a rousing introduction, which the candidate fed of off immediately. Harrison declared, "The story that I ever said one dollar a day was enough for a workingman, with all its accompaniments and appendages, is not a perversion of anything I ever said—*it is a false creation.*" He also denied charges of bigotry: "I will only add that it is equally false that anywhere at any time I ever spoke disparagingly of my fellow-citizens of Irish nativity or descent." He then tied his antibigot sensitivities to his stance on a high protective tariff: "Many of them are now enrolling themselves on the side of protection for American labor—this created the necessity for the story." Illuminating the Republican's educational campaign, he finished by stating, "I want to say again that those who pitch a campaign upon so low a level, greatly underestimate the intelligence, the sense of decency, and the love of fair play of the American people." The talk may have been one of the more influential of the season. An Albany newspaper editor informed Harrison: "The politics of New York City, as a rule, are the politics of Albany 24 hours later. Here in the capital, the political center, the indication that reaches me from every section of the state warrants the prediction that we will win and by a very decisive majority."[36] While Harrison's dramatic rebuttals were reprinted for all of the voters to read, Cleveland remained mum, despite rumors about his alleged pro-English trade leanings and stories that had existed for years about an alleged sex act that he had committed while living in Buffalo.

While some folks came to Indianapolis for a positive celebration, others came ready to be rowdy and commit illegal acts. Drunkenness and pickpocketing were crimes that sometimes occurred on the train ride into town and also during the gatherings. These early problems must have been ominous signs for Harrison's campaign strategists as well. After the Prohibitionist success in 1884, Republicans added an antiliquor plank to their platform in 1888. As Richard Jensen has written, "In the 1880s, in state after state the Republican Party was taken over by aggressive pietists who demanded prohibition and restrictions on parochial schools." Throughout the summer, the campaign did its best to provide hoopla and spectacle without too much drunken debauchery. Sometimes it worked out; other times the rowdiness got out of control. It does not appear that tales of alcohol consumption and bad behavior motivated people to vote for a Prohibitionist over the Republican though. In September, Clarkson received a letter from a Republican operative in Indianapolis: "I find the Methodist ministers very active for Harrison. Prohibition is not very formidable." The chair of the Iowa Republican State Committee, Charles Beardsley, also wrote to Clarkson: "I have investigated the prohibition movement with considerable thoroughness, sending out about 500 letters of inquiry and receiving responses from nearly all counties." From this he speculated, "The present indications are that the Prohibition vote will not be more than it was in 1884, when it reached 1400. We are securing the names and post-offices of all these third party men and will bring to bear upon them the most effective influences."[37]

It appears that the key to understanding the historical significance of the bad behavior on display in Indianapolis is not the behavior itself, but it is the keen ability of Republican strategists to bury any such stories on a national level. Despite the cantankerous nature of some groups and individuals, most of the national press did not report on the fighting, stabbings, pickpockets, and drunken melees in Indianapolis. They did not allow the crime to ruin the overall national image of the events. Occasionally, sheets such as the *Chicago Tribune,* the *Cleveland Plain Dealer,* and the *Saint Louis Dispatch* did let their readers know about some rough patches in the Indiana capital, but they did not consistently report the problems or make a big deal about their potential influence on voters' perceptions of the Republican Party. None of the tales of debauchery appeared in important organs in the swing state of New York, such as the *New York Herald,* a pro-Democratic organ by 1888, or the *New York Times,* another Democratic sheet. But the chances of voters in Indiana knowing about the level of rowdiness in the city were higher because of word of mouth and the penchant that both the *Indianapolis Sun* and the *Indianapolis Sentinel* had for shedding light on some of these problems. Despite some of the reports, not enough of the bad news made it out nationally to hurt Harrison's brand enough to cost him the election.

Most newspapers also helped the campaign by keeping rumors about Harrison's declining health out of the news. One Republican sheet insisted that the candidate was in "robust health," but a Democratic sheet countered that Harrison was "physically and politically played out" just two weeks into the front porch campaign. It seems that evidence from those close to the candidate favored the Democratic view, but many of these anecdotes were generally kept quiet. Some of his friends warned Harrison about the perils of front porch campaigning from both the political and personal side, one declaring, "If you were under my command as of old, I should say steady—no speeches—no letters—we will carry you through." Another confidant wrote to him just a few weeks into the campaign to "be careful—the enemy are watching and will misconstrue most anything you can say, and we are afraid, too, that your health may suffer." On July 21 the Associated Press representative who followed Harrison, Charles Hedges, contended that the candidate might "utterly collapse before the campaign is over." He also noted that the Republican had "grown cross and ill-tempered even to those of his family." Hedges reported that the candidate was "exceedingly sensitive regarding the subject of his health and his staying powers, and at times persistently resists his physician, his family, and the Central Committee in their efforts to hold him in check and save his strength. Chairman Huston privately thinks the General has not more than one half the vital energy he had the day he was nominated; this loss of strength is largely due to the earnestness with which he does everything, thus employing his nervous as well as his muscular system."[38] Not only were these opinions largely kept from the press and the voters, but Harrison's personal health and emotional issues also never crept to the surface during his public speeches or interactions with his visitors. For Republicans in this campaign, message control proved to be as significant as the message itself.

In addition to the speeches, celebrations, drunkenness, and gift exchanges, Harrison's front porch strategy also involved a great deal of close, personal contact—much of it in the form of incessant handshaking. Harrison claimed that he liked to squeeze his visitors' hands first so they could not grasp his own too tightly. Standing on a platform and reaching down to his visitors with both hands at once, the general averaged, by one estimate, "over sixty shakes a minute." While the ritual certainly helped personalize the visit for Harrison's followers, his detractors took pleasure in criticizing him for it. One Democrat reasoned that the Republican loved shaking hands because it was the best way to show that he was not cold and aristocratic. A crowd would visit Harrison, who preplanned on not shaking hands, and the candidate would see a Civil War veteran and insist on a shake; the "jig was up" then, and he would have to shake everybody's hand in the delegation. The *New York Herald* referred to his handshaking style as "the customary pump handle exercises." *Harper's Weekly* laid out a negative historical perspective on the behavior. The magazine posited that even when a man received the nomination for the presidency, "he still has his own business to take care of." The constant handshaking thus seemed like "a wholly unnecessary torture for a Presidential candidate." William Henry Harrison had faced a barrage of handshakes on his way to Washington, DC, which had contributed to his declining health when he arrived at the capital. Also, *Harper's* noted that George Washington refused handshaking opportunities when he served as president.[39] Handshaking and speechmaking were where spectacle and educational politics truly crossed over.

Harrison's newly personable style was equally engineered to endear him to former enemies as well as current political opponents. In one instance a group of 201 Democrats visited the Republican. One of them bet another that he would never actually be able to meet the candidate. The *Indianapolis Sun* reported that not only did the man have the chance to meet Harrison but also "had an agreeable chat" with him. Whether partisanship was in decline by 1888 or not, every expert agreed that the presidential election that year would be a close contest, so a positive visit like this might have helped Harrison with voters on the fence or equally may have hurt him with his base. In another fascinating interlude, a former Confederate officer from Tennessee approached the candidate inside his home, saying, "I was not with you from 61 to 64 . . . but I am now."[40] While Garfield's campaign in 1880 yielded no known instances of public post–Civil War reconciliation, eight years later Harrison found himself publicly reconciling with a former Confederate soldier inside his own home. Now Republicans were not only willing to share their homes with their wives as partners with a say, but the Republican presidential candidate was also shaking hands and exchanging pleasantries with an ex-Confederate soldier.

Harrison's front porch campaign did much to help personalize him for the electorate, in the process making him more likable and, ultimately, more electable. Pro-Democratic newspapers, sensing the danger of the campaign's success, criticized him for his methods. The *New York Herald* declared one Harrison speech "a good deal like picnic lemonade. It is cooling, diluted, abundant—with nothing to affect the morals or the health of the most innocent." The *Cleveland Plain Dealer* posited that the candidate was "in perfect misery" while he met the masses who called on him daily. On one occasion the *Saint Louis Dispatch* referenced Harrison with the headline "GRANDPA'S BOY BEN." The sheet even conjectured that the Republican National Committee had asked the candidate to "quit talking so much" and joked that he would gain 100,000 votes if put into "temporary retirement." Despite such criticism, Republican sheets across the United States continued to heap praise on the general for his ability during his speeches to connect with all classes of men, to personalize his talks for each audience, and to avoid making mistakes. On Election Day Harrison received a letter from Senator Blaine commending him for his series of performances: "No man living could poll a larger Republican vote than you will receive Tuesday. I believed so before you were nominated. Every day of the campaign has confirmed my belief. Every word you have spoken has strengthened your position and you have not by commission or omission weakened yourself a tittle in any direction."[41] Like Garfield, Harrison did not commit any major blunders for his opponents to exploit during his speeches or his interludes with visitors while making himself a unifying candidate for Republicans.

Harrison's public appearances made for a telling contrast to his opponent's refusal to campaign actively. Siding with the traditional maxim that "the office sought the man," President Cleveland chose to maintain a laissez-faire style. The *Buffalo Express* asked their "Democrat brethren" two questions: "Why is it that no delegations of their party care enough for Cleveland to come great distances to offer him congratulations and pledge him loyal support? Why is it that Harrison's speeches are read with delight and Cleveland's mouth is padlocked?" For the *Express,* the answers seemed obvious: Harrison was a free choice for voters while Cleveland was a necessity, and Harrison's ideas "spring forth fresh and vigorous from a brain teaming with crisp, incisive, pithy thoughts" while Cleveland had to "rummage in the musty and dusty leaves of an encyclopedia for ideas." In chorus with the *Express,* the *Philadelphia American* posited that while Harrison addressed the people "without the smallest loss of personal dignity on his part," he could not "talk so much and say so little as the President did at the Virginia University commencement this summer." At a time when Harrison made the most of the tariff issue, as Calhoun has pointed out, Cleveland "failed to dispel popular anxieties aroused by Republican warnings against free-trade. He reserved consideration of more down-to-earth issues such as the tariff for the one substantive statement he made during the campaign, his formal letter of acceptance. . . . adhering to notions of political decorum, Cleveland stood for the presidency in 1888; he did not run." Cleveland could have given speeches clarifying his position on the hottest issue in the campaign, but he chose to remain silent. As H. Wayne Morgan has written, "He remained a figure. Not a man." Cleveland himself admitted that he lacked personal charisma: "No, I have no style, I simply say what is in my mind and seems to be necessary at the time, and say it in my blundering way, and that is all there is to it." While Cleveland may have had no style, in 1888 the Democrats were changing styles and running an educational campaign. Examples of such efforts, as McGerr has shown, include one Connecticut Democratic club formed "for the purpose of doing hard and honest work and not to enjoy themselves in torchlight parades and banquets" and another club in Wisconsin whose president promised "to abstain from such methods of campaigning as address themselves to the excitement of the emotions rather than educating or convincing the intelligence of our citizens. Torchlight processions, bonfires and all appeals to the emotions rather than to the judgment of men are to be barred."[42] Even with this new stress on a more intellectual campaign style, many of the problems that were reported on the streets of Indianapolis were precipitated by Republicans *and* Democrats behaving boorishly toward each other.[43] Nationally in 1888, Democrats were shifting toward educational campaigning, but in Indiana they were still engaged in spectacle politics.

The Republican candidate's crowds may have been raucous and controversial in the press, but his front porch campaign was important in helping him win the election of 1888. It is true, as Calhoun has written, that the results were "so close and the variables so numerous it is impossible to explain Harrison's victory with precision or assurance."[44] Harrison received 5,443,892 popular votes and amassed 233 electoral votes by winning twenty states, while Cleveland garnered 5,534,488 votes and tallied 168 electoral votes from eighteen states. Technically, Harrison became the first candidate to win a presidential election after losing the popular vote but winning the Electoral College outright.[45] The two swing states in the election were Indiana and New York—both had voted for Cleveland in the close race of 1884, but both switched to the Republican four years later.

Harrison's Hoosier support was, nevertheless, not universal. In the state's seventeen southernmost counties, he lost to the Democrat by roughly 3,500 votes. His support was stronger—but still close—in the state's twenty-eight western counties, where he won the popular vote with 70,632 to Cleveland's 69,956. Indiana's twelve northern counties favored the Republican by a tally of 36,658 to 34,590. Ironically, Harrison lost the one county in which his face-to-face campaign style might have been expected to help him the most—Indianapolis's Marion County.[46] Did the front porch campaign alienate the voters who felt most strongly its effect on their daily lives? Perhaps the overcrowding, drunkenness, noise, and fighting swayed the locals toward Cleveland. But the press record (even in the reportage of Democratic-leaning papers) does suggest convincingly that Harrison ingratiated himself to every visiting delegation from elsewhere in the state, so the front porch campaign may have helped him win Indiana and, with it, the Electoral College and therefore the presidency. Processions, gift giving, and incessant handshaking seemed silly to some observers, even at the time. But along with the many other details of this very public and very personal campaign, they went a long way toward making Harrison more likable to the electorate, both in the key swing state of Indiana and beyond.

CHAPTER 3

The Pen, the Press, and the Platform

William McKinley's Fabled Front Porch Campaign

On October 9, 1896, Republican campaign organizers were able to promote a unique scene in US political history as part of the biggest front porch campaign yet. The Union Veterans Patriotic League from Cleveland accompanied several other veterans' organizations to welcome a group of ex-Confederate soldiers coming to Canton, Ohio, by train from Virginia to see the Republican nominee, former Union officer William McKinley. When the southerners started piling out of their trains, the northerners gave them a "lusty, deep throated Yankee salute." The ex-Confederates replied with a "rebel yell fresh from Dixie" as they formed a column next to their old enemies. With the Stars and Stripes flowing above them, the two lines quickly blurred into one as the antagonists from the 1860s hugged each other "like long lost brothers." As one newspaper put it, "Men who had fought their way from Manassas to Appomattox were extolling Stonewall Jackson and Phil Sheridan in a single breath."[1] The former soldiers paraded down the streets of Canton together on their way to hear a presidential candidate tell them about the importance of Americans patriotically sticking together to protect their homes, wives, and children amid the worst depression in US history.

These were precisely the kinds of events that McKinley's campaign managers, including the famed Mark Hanna, loved to generate and market across America to millions of voters through the newspapers. McKinley's front porch campaign dwarfed Harrison's as 750,000 people traveled to Canton, Ohio, and listened to the candidate's message of class unity, a protective tariff, and maintaining the gold standard. In opposition to that Republican message, the People's Party (also known as the Populists) had formed in 1892 to protect the interests of farmers and working-class people. Many members of the party employed divisive class rhetoric in their speeches, highlighting the wealth of the haves and the number of the have-nots in American society as a result of industrialization. They espoused much more government exertion in the economy, including a graduated income tax, government control over railroads, and a change from the traditional gold standard to a gold/silver standard for backing currency. The Populists called for far more government action than Republicans were willing accept, which changed the party's rhetoric about protecting the home and domestic ideals. Before the birth of Populism, Republicans protected home ideals through government activity, particularly high tariffs and Union pensions. By 1896 they claimed to protect homes against too much government interference. By the mid-1890s, Rebecca Edwards has posited, both major parties described male protection of the home as a block to the "violent physical threat" posed by an enlarged, draconian federal government.[2] An effective front porch campaign from another small midwestern "island community" could do much to help Republicans merchandize their brand as the party of hearth, home, and family protection.

The Populists were not the only new enemy for Republicans in 1896. Upper-class and middle-class party members feared that labor unrest threated their homes as well. Throughout the 1880s and into the 1890s, Republicans portrayed Democratic policies as a threat to labor; now frustrated workers were the threat. Incidents such as the Haymarket Riot, Coxey's March on Washington, the Homestead Strike, the Coeur d'Alene incident, and the Pullman Strike made Republican homeowners and families nervous. American families were afraid of "mob rule," or the "mobocracy," as the press dubbed malcontented laborers. By the mid-1890s, Republican leaders who advertised themselves as "men of law and order" warned against disgruntled workers and offered to protect law-abiding families from the "criminal riffraff."[3] The law-and-order label made it even more essential for the party to run a front porch campaign devoid of campaign hooliganism and full of safe, organized visits to McKinley's home and family.

Importantly, a large part of McKinley's success was also his party's ability to include many different kinds of Americans into the family atmosphere generated in Canton. The candidate's own family effectively connected with other prominent Republican families during the campaign, creating a large, family-like atmosphere at the top of the ticket. Besides working-class white men, other groups—including African American male voters from the North, female voters from the West, naturalized citizens from Europe, first-time voters, and Civil War veterans from both the Union and even some from the Confederacy—came to Canton to be a part of the Republican family as well. McKinley offered all of the nonwhite and female groups the same false promises and platitudes that his predecessors did. During the process, he managed to effectively personalize himself to a national audience as well as carefully control not only the message that his speeches gave through newspapers but also the image of a campaign promoting an orchestrated, organized family atmosphere. This proved to be tricky as criminal riffraff, organizational issues, overcrowding troubles, and boorish behavior sometimes occurred over the summer. But Republican managers and editors kept most of these events out of their newspapers, allowing Canton to be a Republican Mecca mostly devoid of crime, well organized, and replete with law-abiding families enjoying spectacle politics while being educated on the issues. Historians have highlighted the effective job that McKinley's campaign did of publishing his speeches verbatim through the press for a national audience. Yet among the myriad of daily challenges that organizers faced in 1896, maybe their most important, underrated job was to orchestrate events that brought diverse swaths of voters to McKinley's home to properly merchandize their candidate's cozy image with various Americans in what would be a close contest.

In July 1896 the Democrats nominated a party supporter, William Jennings Bryan, after he gave a magnificent speech at the Chicago convention. A Populist supporter, Bryan espoused a change from the gold standard to a gold/silver standard to back the paper dollar. The thirty-six-year-old "Boy Orator" from Lincoln, Nebraska, had a remarkable way with words. He fused the religious imagery that he used as a preacher with political and economic rhetoric aimed at framing the angry, unemployed masses versus a small, successful upper class. Bryan's class antagonism and religious fervor could be felt at the convention center and around the country as he closed his famous "Cross of Gold" speech. In reference to the Republican Party's stance that a gold standard should be maintained, Bryan sneered: "You shall not press down upon the brow of labor this crown of thorns. You shall not crucify humanity upon a cross of gold!" Following the convention, Bryan embarked on a national speaking tour of over half of the country by train.[4] His stops inspired hundreds of thousands of "common men" to come out of their homes and listen to the Boy Orator talk from the back of his train. People soon labeled Bryan a "political evangelist."

A friend of the Democratic candidate wrote to him, "I want to say that no matter what may be the result, you will be greater than any other man since Christ."[5] Such evaluations of Bryan surely made Republican planners nervous and thoughtful about how to electioneer against him.

Just about the only characteristic that Bryan and McKinley shared was their first name. McKinley was born in 1843 in Niles, Ohio. He dropped out of college due to his family's financial trouble, then enlisted in the Union army following Fort Sumter (rising from the ranks to be breveted a major by the end of the war). McKinley started practicing law in Canton in 1866. Following a decade of law practice, he successfully campaigned for the House of Representatives in 1876. He had started developing a reputation for being warm and personable on the campaign trail, earning a reputation as a persuasive speaker for the tariff once in Washington. In 1890 McKinley was defeated for reelection, but the "McKinley Bill" passed through Congress that year raised the tariff schedule and made his last name nationally recognized. As the decade wore on, he became known as the "Napoleon" of protection. Despite the moniker, McKinley seemed likable to almost everyone he met as a politician and served as governor of Ohio from 1891 to 1895. As the Republican national convention approached in 1896, McKinley seemed to straddle the issue of silver because he favored maintaining the gold standard in front of conservative crowds but supported silver in front of "inflationist" crowds. As one author has posited, "This may have indicated to some that he was weak on principal, but it demonstrated that he was shrewd in politics."[6]

On the surface the Republican convention and campaign did not seem like "political evangelism" at all. The party wanted to stick with the gold standard and supported a high protective tariff. Its leaders decided who the nominee would be at their convention; there were no speeches from potential candidates. McKinley held true to political custom and did not attend the convention nor make any speeches to try to garner support; he was notified that he was the nominee while at home in Canton.[7] At this point McKinley faced a campaign decision. In 1880 and 1888 Garfield and Harrison had successfully employed the front porch technique to win their respective elections.[8] Should he stump for the presidency like Bryan? Should he stay at home and give speeches from his front porch like his Republican predecessors? Or should he stay quiet like the Founding Fathers would have?

McKinley knew that Bryan would show him up if he went on a cross-country speaking tour. The Republican candidate famously said to a campaign manager who suggested that he stump: "If I should go now it would be an acknowledgment of weakness. Moreover, I might just as well put up a trapeze on my front lawn and compete with some professional athletes as go out speaking against Bryan. I have to *think* when I speak." McKinley also preferred not to leave his home because his wife was an invalid and could not travel with him. Reporters described the candidate's tastes as "simple" and that his major weakness was his penchant for cigars, "in which he rivals General Grant in the number of strong black cigars smoked every day." McKinley was not "exactly a fluent talker," but he could "tell an interesting story" and always prepared his speeches ahead of time. On speechmaking, he said: "When I have an important speech to make it absorbs me. It is hard work and it takes all there is in me. I go over the subject again and again in all its phases in my mind. I read all I can get hold of upon it. . . . I dictate it to my stenographer and see that the copy is given out beforehand. This clarifies my thought." When asked if he liked to give speeches, McKinley emphatically replied: "No, I do not. I dread it. My heart goes down into my boots whenever I get up before an audience, and I tremble until I have begun to talk. This is always so, and still I have been making speeches for 28 years."[9]

Despite his personal distaste for speeches, McKinley began talking just hours after he received word of his nomination. His organizers began setting up processions to his home just after the news reached Canton, three weeks before Bryan gave his "Cross of Gold" speech. In contrast, immediately following the Democratic convention, Bryan started stumping from the back of trains, eventually traveling over 18,000 miles, giving a total of 600 speeches, and averaging speaking 80,000 words a day.[10] Bryan's activity made the front porch campaign in Canton even more important. McKinley's handlers knew that a nation of newsreaders, in the middle of the worst depression they had ever experienced, wanted to see some activity from their presidential candidates. With Bryan appearing so dynamic, McKinley could not seem aloof or sedentary. The Democrats seemed even more threatening when Republican staff started receiving news that Bryan appealed to voters who supported bimetallism in key states in the Midwest and the West. Fear of losing the election to a more active candidate with a radical idea motivated McKinley's handlers to turn Canton into a Republican Mecca and enlarge the front porch campaign.

Mark Hanna proved to be just the right man for the creative task of helping McKinley take on Bryan. Born into a business family in Lisbon, Ohio, Hanna had displayed a flair for dramatic planning when he organized a burlesque show during his sophomore year of college; he was suspended and never returned.[11] Hanna briefly served the Union during the Civil War and then went on to become a business mogul in Cleveland. He was a major player in the city's coal, iron, electric, gas, and transit industries as well as the owner of an opera house, a bank, and numerous companies. He organized a marching club there in support of Garfield in 1880.[12] In the 1880s Hanna transitioned from city to state politics and began gaining political power in northern Ohio. Republicans began referring to him as "Uncle Mark," the "Red Boss," and "Captain Hanna" as he controlled Cleveland and Ohio politicians from behind closed doors with his fund-raising abilities, personal and business connections, and his own wealth. Throughout the decade, the Red Boss shifted between backing Joe Foraker and John Sherman for political leadership in the Buckeye State. Hanna became impressed by McKinley at the 1888 Republican nominating convention when the congressman remained loyal to Sherman's bid for the nomination despite some delegates' calls for his own elevation. In 1891 and 1893 Hanna helped McKinley win Ohio's gubernatorial race and two years later stopped working in the private sector to devote himself entirely to McKinley's potential 1896 bid for the presidency.[13]

In 1896 Hanna demonstrated that he believed in educational campaigning at least as much as James Clarkson had eight years previously. The scale of the Red Boss's newspaper efforts outdid those of any previous campaign manager from either party. It was made possible because he was able to raise record amounts of donations, in part because of his money-generating capabilities and also because Bryan scared the moneyed elite with his class antagonism from the stump. Hanna raised over $3,500,000 to put together the largest educational campaign apparatus in US political history. He established campaign headquarters in both New York City and Chicago. In the Windy City, Republican leadership also set up a Speakers' Bureau, a Literary Bureau, and departments for relations with African Americans, laborers, Scandinavians, Germans, college students, and even traveling salesmen. A Chicago businessman named Charles Dawes ran this large-scale apparatus by adopting the business practices of railroad and utility companies. The Statistical Department prepared pro-Republican stories for newspapers across the country. The Literary Bureau produced over 275 different pamphlets about economic issues, such as the tariff and the gold standard, appearing in twenty-one different languages. All told, the campaign produced 220 million copies, or more than a dozen for each American voter. One newspaper noted, "Never before . . . has there been such an incessant bombardment of the public mind and conscience by leaflets, pamphlets and reprints of arguments by public men and economic authorities."[14] While Chicago and New York served as the twin epicenters of Hanna's educational campaign, Canton was the theater for McKinley's spectacle.

In the fall of 1805, James Leonard surveyed and plotted Canton. The next year he purchased a lot and erected the first building in the area, which stood until 1879. In 1815 the settlement's population reached nearly five hundred people, and a group of businessmen established a local bank to help support the growing economy. Also that year the *Canton Repository* began publication. On January 30, 1822, Canton officially became incorporated as a town and received mail two to three times a week by stagecoach. That year its government issued one ordinance to "preserve cleanliness and promote safety" and another "to regulate the market and extinguish fire." In March 1838 the Ohio legislature divided Canton into four wards and created a town council, consisting of a mayor, a recorder, and two members from each ward. In 1854 the town became a village, and its council changed Canton into "a city of the second class." Between 1868 and 1886 the city experienced a series of fires at local businesses.[15]

Canton in 1896 had 198 businesses that produced 6,000 different products shipped throughout the United States and internationally. The city had nine banks, five of them savings establishments. The local paper pointed out that Canton was the perfect town to back a candidate who espoused a high protective tariff to protect domestic manufacturers as well as a sound money policy.[16] Having 86 passenger trains that went through the city on a daily basis, Canton grew from 12,258 people in 1880 to 26,180 in 1890. Six years later the population had increased to 40,492, which made Canton the sixth-largest city in Ohio.[17]

The city's economy prospered from the booming business brought by the visiting throngs. Some locals prominently displayed a sign on Main Street that stated, "There will be better times. Buy a buggy." A train butcher shouted out from his caboose, "Chewing Gum and McKinley Buttons." In front of one building, a shoe-store owner's sign read, "Sure winners—McKinley and F's Shoes." A fish salesman had a picture of the candidate displayed next to his fish, while a grocer planted a McKinley banner inside a dried apple barrel at his store. W. D. Caldwell & Company sold McKinley souvenir spoons for $2.00 each. Saloons sold a drink combination of bourbon, tea, and sugar dubbed a "McKinley." The local Western Union Office increased its telegraphic workforce from four men to eleven after its daily workload increased from 1,000 words to 20,000 words. Postmaster John Monnet claimed to be selling stamps at a rate of $62,000 a year, while the much larger cities of Akron and Youngstown averaged $40,000 a year. The *Cleveland Plain Dealer* snidely remarked that local churches had briefly entered into the restaurant business by feeding and charging visitors. Many residents made the campaign a part of their household. George Foster trained his parrot to say "McKinley"—when news of the nomination reached Canton, the town's new gong started going off, and the parrot started screaming "McKinley" over and over again, apparently "with all its might."[18] The Republican front porch campaign undoubtedly injected life into a sputtering local economy and helped mollify some of the downtrodden emotions that came with a dismal business environment.

Seemingly, Hanna and his fellow campaign managers did turn the small Ohio city into a destination for Republicans. Historians estimate that, between June 19 and November 2, a total of 750,000 people visited Canton in three hundred delegations from thirty states, stretching from Vermont to New Mexico. Railroads cut to $3.50 the roundtrip fare from Chicago to Canton, which made it "cheaper than staying at home." The rail companies reported bringing 9,000 cars filled with visiting delegations for McKinley to the Ohio city. They provided even lower discounts to groups that had more than forty folks. On one mid-September Saturday, roundtrip tickets from Chicago to Canton were reduced to $1.00. To keep everything flowing smoothly, McKinley's organizers put together thirteen committees, one each for finance, invitations, reception and escort, music and program, decorations, parades, speakers, hotels and accommodations, advertisements and press, fireworks, carriages and conveyances, and transportation. The thirteenth, the Committee for Arrangements, planned where the processions would march on their way to McKinley's house and where they would stand to hear him speak; if bad weather prevailed, then they went to an indoor facility called the Tabernacle to hear the candidate. Delegations walked from the train station down Main Street under the McKinley Arch, which campaign planners created. The young men who made up the McKinley Home Guard would find out which delegation was coming next and ride ahead to tell the candidate so that he could tailor his remarks accordingly. As during the Harrison campaign, the speeches that delegation leaders made to introduce McKinley were vetted to avoid unchoreographed or uncomfortable moments. The candidate apparently sat on a stage and listened to each introduction "like a child looking at Santa Claus." After his own remarks, McKinley invited his visitors to come into his home and shake his hand. One sheet described the house as "modest" but effective for entertaining visitors because of rooms built on either side of the main entrance hallway. Usually, McKinley entertained men in the north parlor, while women occupied the south room. When the candidate introduced visitors to his mother with pride, the gesture was clearly not politically motivated.[19]

Historians have stressed the primacy of highly partisan newspapers in making McKinley's campaign activities known to the nation. Reporters were given the candidate's prepared speeches to reprint so that millions of Americans could read them the day after he spoke. The largest processions were intentionally planned for Saturday so that McKinley's words would appear in Sunday papers nationwide. The campaign prepared a special tent for the press, in which reporters who drank alcohol were given one sandwich and two beers, while those who did not were offered a cup of coffee and two sandwiches. The *Chicago Tribune* relayed a telling story about McKinley's success in garnering the support of so many papers. A longtime Democrat in Canton had his son go buy him a copy of his favorite political newspaper. Upon reading the editorial page, the older man discovered the sheet's endorsement of McKinley. He sent his son out for an exchange of papers, and the new sheet also endorsed the Republican, to which the man asked his son, "Has McKinley captured all the papers?" The *Toledo Blade* opined that the popular Republican's speeches proved to be "those of a modest and sincere man, and show him to be [a] level-headed" candidate whose "simple, sincere, old-fashioned way of addressing his hearers . . . makes a far more favorable impression than all the arts of the elocutionist [Bryan]." Recently, one author has contended that the Ohioan's campaign style was more effective than Bryan's whirlwind train tour. The Boy Orator would sleep for intermittent periods of time, then wake up and speak extemporaneously from the back of his train while reporters struggled to write down every word he said; thus many of his speeches were printed incompletely in newspapers. Bryan may have been the more spectacular orator, but the cohesion of McKinley's campaign with the press ensured that his remarks in their entirety reached millions of voters.[20] These factors combined to help Republicans merchandise their candidate's speeches more effectively than his opponent's. Additionally, accompanying the text of his speeches were often stories about McKinley's interactions with the many different kinds of visitors and the delegations' interactions with each other and the locals. Collectively taken, these reports portrayed a strong sense of solidarity among the many various people in Canton around the idea of protecting American homes, families, and businesses. These scenes were critical in Hanna's attempts at image control and effectively branding his candidate as the man for protecting those ideals.

Projecting family-like togetherness at the top of the Republican ticket proved to be an effective marketing technique. The candidate's wife and mother were both prominent from their respective front porch. On the way to the candidate's home, visitors paraded by his mother's house. At eighty-seven years old, Nancy Allison McKinley would sit out on her front porch for about an hour in the morning and acknowledge the passing throngs. His wife, Ida Saxton McKinley, was a consistently prominent part of his own public appearances. The *Chicago Tribune* noted: "She is almost her husband's shadow. He is never out of her sight." Before speaking, the candidate would "almost invariably give her a nod and a smile."[21] Despite her health issues, Ida played the same important role that the spouses of previous front porch candidates played—helping their husbands publicly project a strong family image through the support of their wives. And in McKinley's case, he had his mother to promote this image as well.

Other prominent Republican party members also visited McKinley to show support. On one occasion Harriet S. Blaine, widow of the 1884 Republican candidate and Maine senator, visited McKinley and proclaimed, "hearty congratulations to yourself and Mrs. McKinley, with tender thoughts of the past." She was joined by Lucretia Garfield, who stated, "Our two families unite in congratulations to you and Mrs. McKinley and in the earnest hope that the next four years may bring to you the most of joy and the least of sorrow." Other family members of former Republican candidates also visited the home in Canton, including the son of Rutherford Hayes and two sons of Garfield, one of them now a senator from Ohio. When McKinley addressed a group from the late president's Nineteenth Congressional District of Ohio, he gave "what was principally a eulogy to Garfield." Gift giving to the presidential candidate was even connected to prominent Republican Party members. In one instance McKinley received an attractive gold-mounted cane that was partly made from a cupboard located in Senator Blaine's home.[22] These interactions, statements, and gifts were made known to voters around the United States to emphasize the family-like environment that existed even among those connected to the very top of the Republican ticket.

Not only did the front porch campaign bring national Republican leadership together, but also state and local Republican leaders and organizers coordinated, making public appearances with each other and centralizing behind a strong candidate as an integrated political unit. The various local Republican committees, as well as the state committee, were in constant coordination with those from other states and localities to arrange the timing and nature of such visits. Congressmen and governors from various states met each other in Canton and made public appearances together behind McKinley on his front porch. The *Cleveland Plain Dealer* labeled one early fall day in town "governor's day" as the chief executives of Vermont, Rhode Island, and Ohio all came together to support McKinley.[23] While the candidate encouraged Americans to come together, Republican leadership mirrored his message onstage as they stood behind him.

Just as in 1880 and 1888, bringing first-time voters into the Republican fold would be important in such a tight, partisan atmosphere. Such voters may have been even harder to attract than usual for Republicans in 1896, given the youthful age of their opponent. Nevertheless, several "First Voters" groups descended upon Canton. One called the McKinley First Voters, from Bowling Green, Kentucky, came to town in September. A month later the First Voters Republican Club from Cleveland made the town feel like a university experiencing a football championship night. According to the *Cleveland Plain Dealer,* other delegations came to Canton throughout the day but did not generate nearly as much excitement as this group of eight hundred young men who, upon arrival, "simply owned the town and treated the vanquished Cantonese as conquerors might treat a defeated foe." Led by a loud, gaudy-looking band called the Great Westers, the group marauded right up to and past McKinley's backyard as a group of Pennsylvania visitors, already on the yard, gawked at them. As if they were a military dispatch, the Clevelanders marched "many" blocks beyond the home, then quickly double backed, countermarched, and "swept" into McKinley's backyard, "sending the Pennsylvanians scattering over the fences and occupying the best position any delegation had yet secured." The *Plain Dealer* criticized the organizational abilities of the Republicans and extolled the first voters' crowd skills simultaneously when they reported, "The crowd applauded the well-executed maneuvers and the success of a little military spirit on a scene where hesitation and lack of management have spoiled many a delegation's need of what they have the right to expect."[24]

These skilled, first-time voters from Cleveland were taken seriously by McKinley when he addressed them. The candidate tried to make them feel important by contending, "You are given the ballot at a time when its use for good or evil to the country was never greater." McKinley explained the broad implications of adopting a gold/silver standard: "No nation can hold its standing before mankind that will depreciate its own currency any more

The arrival of visitors to Garfield's Lawnfield home in Mentor. The small number depicted indicates that this was part of phase one of this first front porch campaign.

ARRIVAL OF VISITORS.

GEN! GARFIELD'S POST OFFICE

GEN! GARFIELDS TELEGRAPHIC OFFICE.

In the foreground is candidate Garfield's telegraph office, located just behind his home. In the background is Mentor's post office.

In the corridor of his home, Garfield appears to be meeting and collaborating with Republican supporters or strategists.

IN THE CORRIDOR

GENL. GARFIELDS CONSULTATION OFFICE.

Candidate Garfield in his consultation room with his secretary and telegraph operator, Joseph Stanley-Brown. Garfield nicknamed him the "Hurler of Lightning."

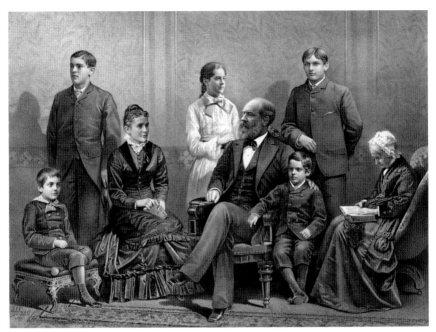

Garfield with his wife (*to his right*), her mother (*to his left*), and his children.

JAMES A. GARFIELD
REPUBLICAN CANDIDATE FOR PRESIDENT

CHESTER A. ARTHUR
REPUBLICAN CANDIDATE FOR VICE PRESIDENT

Presidential candidate Garfield and his vice presidential running mate, Chester Arthur. There is no evidence that Arthur ever visited Garfield at Lawnfield.

Left: Benjamin Harrison around 1888. *Right:* Carolina Harrison was integral to the front porch campaign. Her appearances with her husband helped cement the candidate's image as a family man and softened him in the eyes of the electorate.

The Harrison home. Once the crowds became too large, the candidate started giving his speeches in University Park, down the street from the house.

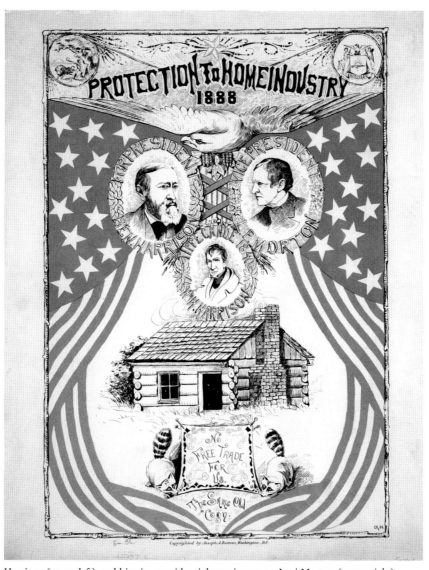

Harrison (*upper left*) and his vice presidential running mate, Levi Morton (*upper right*), appear on the cover of this Republican campaign pamphlet.

An 1888 Democratic pamphlet (about the need to reduce the tariff) features Pres. Grover Cleveland (*left*) and vice presidential running mate Allen Thurman (*right*). The importance and popularity of Frances Folsom, the new wife of the formerly unwed president, is obvious as she appears above and between the two men.

Republican candidate
William McKinley giving
a speech in Canton, Ohio,
to a group of Chicago
Wheelmen in 1896.

McKinley (*left*) on his front porch step with Teddy Roosevelt, his running mate in the 1900 election.

McKinley with his wife (*seated, left*) and his mother (*seated, right*). In the upper left corner is a picture of McKinley's childhood home in Niles, Ohio; in the upper right corner is a picture of his Canton, Ohio, home, from which he conducted his famed front porch campaign in 1896.

McKinley's home in November 1896 after his front porch campaign. Notice the barren lawn, trampled down by the thousands of visitors who came through town.

McKinley relaxing on his front porch in the summer of 1901, shortly after his reelection and just before his assassination.

A 1912 cartoon titled *The Great American Bull-Fight.* The caption underneath the title reads, "When the picadors sufficiently puncture him, the Matador will finish him." The bull being corralled symbolizes Teddy Roosevelt, the Bull Moose Party's candidate. The picador with his back turned (*left*) is Elihu Root, former secretary of state under Roosevelt and secretary of war under Taft, while the bareheaded, white-haired man in front (*right*) is Robert LaFollette, former congressman from and governor of Wisconsin. Woodrow Wilson is the waiting matador in the back. Pres. William Taft is on a horse behind Roosevelt, puncturing his political opponent in the backside with a spear. The race that year saw four candidates tour and stump for the presidency as front porch campaigning started losing its popularity after the turn of the century.

Democratic candidate Woodrow Wilson stumps from the back of a railroad car in 1912.

VOL. LXXII. No. 1861.

PUCK BUILDING, New York, October 30th, 1912.
Copyright, 1912, by Keppler & Schwarzmann. Entered at N. Y. P. O. as Second-class Mail Matter.

PRICE TEN CENTS.

Puck

WOODROW AND THE BEAN-STALK.

Wilson chopping down the beanstalk that supports fat monopolies, sending them tumbling to the ground. From the stump, Wilson articulated a "New Freedom" in which he promised to take down all monopolies in the United States.

Roosevelt stumping from the rear of a train platform as a third-party candidate in 1912.

Warren Harding around 1920.

Suffragettes leaving Washington, DC, in 1920 to head to Harding's home in Marion, Ohio.

Above: The Harding home. The wraparound front porch served the candidate nicely for his speeches.

Left: Florence Harding helped her husband court female voters in 1920, the first time women voted nationally in a presidential election after passage of the Nineteenth Amendment.

than a nation can stand well before the world that will not defend its flag and honor. . . . No nation can command respect at home or abroad if it does not all times uphold the supremacy of law and inviolability of its own sacred obligations." At the end of his remarks, McKinley also tried to make the novices feel like they were equal to seasoned voters: "The ballot of the young man as well as that of the old man; the ballot of the first voter, as well as that of all voters, should always express the voice of truth and conscience. . . . It should embody the highest welfare of himself, his home, his community, and his country. . . . It should express on its face his best hopes and highest aspirations as an individual citizen and always represent the greatest good to his fellow countrymen."[25] The candidate endeared himself to his young followers by making them feel like an equal part of the American family, with a responsibility to the family home to vote for currency maintenance over currency change. Republican newspaper editors and organizers knew that making this type of story available for other first-time voters to read could only help the party's cause.

McKinley and his managers also knew the importance of keeping midwestern and northeastern naturalized voters, nearly all immigrants from Europe, in the Republican fold. They warned that these groups could be financially hampered by the rising prices that would most likely accompany a switch to bimetallism. A few hours before the Cleveland first voters made their presence known in Canton, a group of three hundred Italian Americans of the United Italian Republican Club visited town, having traveled from Pittsburgh. McKinley also received a delegation of twelve hundred Hungarian Americans, a Bohemian delegation from Cleveland, and twelve hundred men from several Polish American clubs from Cleveland. Speaking for the Polish men, William Welfeld exclaimed: "No catiff drove this noble band of Polish citizens to Canton. They came of their free will to express to you, Major McKinley, their loyalty and respect. The Polish are much misrepresented. They love liberty and wherever the battles of freedom have been fought there were the Poles." In another instance, which brought McKinley and ethnic Bohemian voters together, a Bohemian immigrant from Chicago named Thomas Nedved, who could barely speak English, presented a copiously sculpted copper bust of the candidate, for which he had taken off two weeks from his job as a coppersmith to create. McKinley accepted the gift "with pleasure," with newspaper reports making sure to note, "The donor is an ardent McKinley [supporter] and has been engaged in working among citizens of his own nationality for the man of his choice."[26]

Along with first-time and naturalized voters, many different groups of women played an integral part in the spectacle at Canton. A delegation of "old folks," including a "great many elderly women," came one day from Cleveland and several other northeastern Ohio cities. On another occasion several hundred African Americans, "many of them women," from Salem, Massillon, Alliance, and other nearby towns came to visit the candidate. Sometimes the women brought gifts for Mrs. McKinley. Among five hundred ironworkers and steelworkers from Mingo Junction was a large group of women who brought the candidate's wife "a circular floral piece made of chrysanthemums in imitation of a gold dollar. In one side in gold letters were the words 'In God We Trust; November 3, 1896,' and the reverse side was the motto 'Protection and Prosperity, March 4, 1897.'" They also brought a basket of flowers for the candidate's mother.[27]

Other women promised the Republican candidate an even more important gift: their votes. Unlike Garfield and Harrison, McKinley actually met with some women from western states who could cast ballots. A woman named Mrs. Fuller visited from Wyoming and promised that the Republican would receive the vote of "every" female voter in the state. In July, McKinley and his family met with several groups of women from Indiana and Colorado and made remarks tying respect for the gains of women in the public sphere with the process of maintaining stability in American homes: "Practically every avenue of human endeavor is open to her. Her impress is felt in art, science, literature, song and government. Our churches, our schools, our charities, our professions and our general business interests are more than ever directed by her. Respect for womankind has become with us a national characteristic, and what a high and manly trait it is. . . . It stamps the true gentlemen. The man who loves wife and mother and home will respect and reverence all womankind. He is always the better citizen for such gentle breeding." After the talk, a woman from Colorado told McKinley that she would be voting for him and speculated that the ballots of women across the state would deliver its electoral votes to the Republican.[28]

So many women visited McKinley on the day that he received this reassurance, July 15, that one newspaper labeled it "Women's Day" in Canton. The previous day the *Cleveland Plain Dealer* had claimed that the large, planned gathering of women was not a political event or a show of support for Republicans, but instead it was a "personal tribute to Mr. McKinley and his amiable wife." Rain fell throughout the next morning, but the inclement weather did not deter a large group of several hundred Cleveland women from descending upon Canton in the early afternoon. The *Indianapolis Sentinel* described these visitors as leaders in the city's churches, schools, and charities as well as some "with no special claim to distinction." The sheet claimed that the women reflected a "handsome appearance and were very charming in their fresh summer raiment and gay hats, blooming with flowers." Another paper commented that some locals watching the parade thought that the costumes produced "a much finer effect than had the best efforts of the men with all their campaign regalia." The women demonstrated a high degree of organization during their "excellent" parade, and their band, mostly women but with some men, sparked an unusual degree of interest in the audience. The male members played all of the smaller instruments, including the snare drum and the piccolo, while the women played the large, louder instruments, including the base drum.[29] Upon arriving at the McKinley home, a sitting member of the Board of Education in Cleveland, Mrs. Elroy Avery, addressed the gathering in front of the candidate. She also connected his candidacy to protecting the home and simultaneously jabbed the male-dominated American political landscape:

We may not fully appreciate man made political platforms, but we better understand the significance of current events than some folks give us credit for. We know that when . . . the husband lacks work, the wife knows and feels it . . . ; when the factory fires are out, the fire on the hearth burns low; when the spindles cease to turn . . . misery and wailing brood in the home by night. Who shall say that woman has no interest in your success. . . . Among men your name stands as a synonym for protection to American industry. . . . Among women it stands for more than that—it stands for protection for the home, it stands for right thinking and right living, it stands for tenderness to mother and for love to wife, for all that makes the American home the dearest spot on earth, the footprint of God.[30]

When McKinley spoke, he continued talking about the significance of women to American homes and families, tying this continuing domestic development to the maintenance of law and order in American society: "The home over which the trusted wife presides is the citadel of our strength, the best guarantee of good citizenship and sound morals in government. It is the foundation—upon it all else is constructed. From the plain American home, where virtue dwells and truth abides, go forth the men and women who make the great states and cities which adorn our Republic, which maintain law and order." He was said to be more excited than his wife about the basket of roses that the Cleveland delegation presented her.[31] Just like the other porch candidates, McKinley made no specific promises to his female visitors about suffrage nationally and really only provided them lip service, knowing their appearance would help his brand.

The candidate also had personal interactions with these groups that allowed the press to humanize him. When a committee of women came from Cleveland before "Women's Day" to survey the scene in town, a member said of McKinley: "He is the most sympathetic-looking man that I have ever met. We heard him address a delegation of workingmen from Massillon. His words were as full of sympathy and tenderness as a mother could have spoken to her children." She expressed regret to McKinley for his lawn being demolished by all of the visiting throngs, to which he replied, "The people did it, and nothing is too good for the people."[32]

Women could also be aggressive in Canton and were at the center of overcrowding issues during the campaign more than once. About a week after McKinley received news of his nomination, the city's women decided to stage a procession to his home. As one sheet put it, "They came to see McKinley, and see McKinley they would, in spite of police and militia." Authorities stationed two policemen at the head of the steps to the candidate's front porch, two militiamen directly in front of the door to the home, and an "immaculate" lieutenant with a "sweet mustache" and "martial eye-glasses" right in front of the door. The two police officers clasped hands to keep the throng of visitors out while periodically letting "half a score of struggling women get by." The militiamen did the same thing, allowing only a few at a time to enter the residence when the lieutenant said "now." Apparently, "thousands" of women pressed down on the police, as they "had the worst of it," while the militiamen had an easier time because they had to deal with fewer people. The *Chicago Tribune* opined that the militiamen noticeably restrained groups of pretty women with "unusual ardor" and were slower in letting them go.[33]

On another occasion C. S. Lloyd, correspondent for the *Cleveland Plain Dealer,* complained that "the women of course wanted to see all the fun and they refused to leave after the first speech but waited until all the delegations were in and it was all over." He explained that at one point there were twenty families eating lunch in front of McKinley's home in a gigantic, immovable picnic. The crowd around the residence became so dense that several people "were overcome by exhaustion or by the heat." Such conditions affected mostly women, but they "speedily" recovered after being removed from the gathering. Three people required attention from the candidate's personal physician.[34]

Women could also be much louder than their male counterparts while celebrating in Canton. One night it appeared that half the revelers in the streets were women who took "more delight in making the night hideous" than their male counterparts. One paper opined that in Cleveland such behavior would "invite rebuke," but in Canton it appeared to be a "campaign fad."[35] In 1880 in Mentor, women had marched to Garfield's home to hear him explain that he would not comment on women's suffrage because it was not a plank on the Republican platform. Sixteen years later women were much more aggressive and organized in their public campaigning, and some were even able to promise the candidate their vote and those of other women in their state. If women were part of McKinley's American family, then they were at least going to be heard in 1896.

While women and naturalized citizens were making small gains in American society between 1888 and 1896, African Americans were not as Jim Crow laws started permeating the statute books of southern states. Despite this development, Republican managers were determined to promote scenes that demonstrated that blacks were still part of McKinley's American family and that he wanted to protect their homes too. Delegations representing "colored" supporters of McKinley came from New York, Cleveland, Massillon, and other parts of Ohio. The delegation from Cleveland numbered two hundred and came with the L'Ouverture Rifles, a crack African American military organization out of Indiana. They were uniformed in white duck trousers, broadcloth coats, and bearskin shakos. One sheet declared that "they made a fine appearance." McKinley praised the recent gains that he claimed blacks were making in the United States: "I congratulate you, gentlemen, upon the splendid progress that your race has made since emancipation. You have done better; you have advanced more rapidly than it was believed possible at that time; you have improved greatly the education advantages which you have had. Your people everywhere, north and south, are accumulating property and today you stand as among the most conservative of the citizens of this great republic."[36] McKinley and his managers were surely aware of detrimental developments in the South since the early 1890s, but their desire to market Americans as one big, happy family with protected homes under a potential McKinley administration outweighed any desire to publicly state the truth about these troubling racial developments. As with women, McKinley could really only provide lip service to his African American visitors.

Like his predecessors, McKinley also made sure to stage public meetings with fellow Civil War veterans. In 1888 Harrison promised to protect Union veterans' homes and families by protecting their war pensions. By the 1890s groups such as the Sons of Confederate Veterans and the Daughters of Confederate Veterans had started sanitizing the reasons why the South fought by planting monuments commemorating their ancestor's participation in the war and giving speeches laced with "Lost Cause" rhetoric and rationale. The public displays in Canton and meetings with the candidate must have been important for at least some Union veterans to continue to assert their masculinity as victorious soldiers. But others had no problem sharing the spotlight with ex-Confederate soldiers on the day they came to visit; McKinley even brought up the potential of garnering their votes on one occasion. Republican campaign managers used visits from anybody, northern or southern, as critical moments to promote images of solidarity and patriotism through newspapers to counter Bryan's rhetorical habit of pitting classes against each other.

Sometimes Union veterans would bring their families with them to further bolster the family-like atmosphere in Canton. The survivors of the 104th Ohio Volunteer Infantry brought their wives and children with them as well as a Daughters of Veterans group from the local area. Some of the veterans who had visited Garfield in Mentor apparently made a pilgrimage to Canton to see McKinley too. The 23rd Ohio Volunteer Infantry paid a special visit to the candidate; a young, beardless McKinley had been a member of the unit during the Civil War. The candidate became quite emotional when addressing this group, which gave his promoters another opportunity to create dramatic images for readers across the country.[37]

When McKinley spoke to Union veterans, he tied the safety of their pensions to the security of their families and the necessity of maintaining the gold standard to promote sound currency. He used specifics in addressing the issue to three hundred visiting veterans: "There are 970,000 pensioners on the honored pension roll . . . and the government pays out of its public treasury in pensions over $140,000,000 every year to the soldiers and sailors, their widows and orphans. Every dollar of that debt must be paid in the best currency and coin in the world. There is no body in the world more interested in maintaining a sound and stable currency than the old soldiers of the

Republic, their widows, and their orphans." McKinley finished by playing on the men's acute sense of patriotism: "old soldiers this year . . . will stand by the financial honor of the government and will no more permit our nation's integrity to be questioned than they would permit that flag (pointing to an American flag) to be assailed. [Applause and cries of 'You are right.']" Following the speech, he characteristically told the men that he wanted to meet all of them and personally shake their hands. When addressing "old soldiers" in a different instance, McKinley even proposed that the threat of financial dishonor could bring the northern and southern states closer together: "The future is the sacred trust of us all, South as well as North. Honesty, like patriotism, can be bounded by neither State nor sectional lines. Financial dishonor is the threatened danger now, and good men will obliterate old lines of party in a united effort to uphold American honor."[38]

While Harrison had the reputation of being aloof and used his front porch to rehabilitate his image, McKinley seemed to use the spotlight to enhance his already solid reputation. His managers also used the Canton stage to contrast their man's style with that of his opponent. Immediately after Bryan gave a brilliant speech, his train whisked him away to the next town so as many curious onlookers could see the political novelty; few had the chance to personally meet him. McKinley combated this traveling stumping style with solid, mistake-free speeches followed by personable interactions with audience members that involved handshaking, small talk, and accepting gifts from the visitors. These events were covered by and described in newspapers before and after the texts of his speeches.

The all-important ritual handshake between the visitors and the candidate continued in Canton. McKinley may have engaged in more handclasps in 1896 than Harrison and Garfield did in their campaigns combined. One onlooker claimed to have observed the candidate shake hands with a delegation from Cleveland 365 times in ten minutes. On an earlier occasion C. O. L. Cooper, one of the candidate's stenographers, saw a drunk visitor from Buffalo approaching McKinley in front of another delegation. Cooper thought that the man "intended to make a disgusting scene," so he quickly moved behind the candidate and "ran his hand under the Major's arm." He "warmly" shook the drunk's hand, and the man "turned away, perfectly satisfied, and stumbled down the steps and was spirited away." Apparently needing more than a handshake, a man from Pittsburgh at another time came up to McKinley and unexpectedly kissed him "heartily." The kiss surprised him, but the crowd enjoyed the moment and "burst into a storm of cheers." The visitor seemed perfectly satisfied as he marched away with "his face wreathed in smiles."[39] McKinley handled this unvetted, potentially embarrassing moment with ease.

The candidate seemed to have a knack for handling unvetted moments with ease, in the process creating memorable moments for the press to promote. In one telling instance, upon finishing a speech at the Tabernacle, McKinley had to fight his way through a crowd on the way to his carriage. Just before the candidate reached his house, a "boot-blacker" with the "swarthy complexion of a son of sunny Italy" approached his buggy and asked to shine McKinley's shoes. The candidate "alighted," so the young man continued to ask him all the way to his front porch until McKinley finally acquiesced, dropping into a chair and letting the boy shine his shoes while the crowd laughed and applauded his persistence. Just as the interlude ended, McKinley received a gamecock as well as a raccoon caught near his old farm in Columbiana County.[40]

There were several other exchanges with very young visitors that were probably more comfortable for McKinley and really humanized him for a national audience. Once the candidate met a man with his three-year-old son. McKinley clasped hands with the youth, who, "with a fervor and dignity of a voter, said proudly: 'I'm for sound money.'" McKinley appreciated his position and replied, "That's right, my boy." Another time a firefighter from Forest City named Frank Ferrell visited Canton with his wife, five-year-old child, and infant son to see the candidate. McKinley's organizers used the opportunity to stage a nice promotional moment. They allowed Ferrell and his family to go into McKinley's office, where Ferrell placed his son into the candidate's chair so the boy could say that he once sat where the president sat. McKinley personally greeted the "delighted mother." A sheet described that the baby, a "pretty one," smiled at the candidate, who "took one of its chubby little hands in his and spoke kindly to the infant."[41]

In another highly humanizing moment, a friend from the Ohio legislature, Maj. Benjamin Butterworth, recalled visiting with McKinley during the summer of 1896. On their way to church one morning, Butterworth asked the candidate if it exalted him that people from around the world were talking about him. He replied: "No, if it tends to anything it makes me the more sensible of my own shortcomings and to seek with greater earnestness than in my life to learn the way in which my feet should go. Never before . . . have I been so sensible of my own weaknesses." Clearly impressed by McKinley's off-the-cuff honesty, Butterworth told one newspaper, "The remarks were so purely unstudied and his deep religious sense so apparent that one could not help but feel the pathos that always surrounded Lincoln's lonely pathway as he spoke."[42] Capturing these types of interactions, with adults and young people, helped Republican editors personalize and market their candidate even more effectively.

The gift-exchange process also gave McKinley the chance to personalize his interactions with the presenter and the audience that person represented. Harrison started this process in 1888; McKinley perfected it eight years later. As Gil Troy has written, "These gifts attested to the increased centrality of the candidate and the desire of individuals to cement their bond with him." Like Harrison's gifts, McKinley's ranged from symbolic to fascinating to zany. He received a handsome porcelain bathtub decorated in gold leaf from a Pittsburgh manufacturing concern and a gold loving cup from a jewelry firm in New York. He was given a roasted gold ore by a McKinley mining club. The candidate sometimes received symbolic animals as well, among them a bald eagle—the "bird of freedom" as one sheet characterized it—from a California group. McKinley was also presented with a "jet black saddle horse" named Midnight, which he had ridden into the Chicago World's Fair in 1893 to represent Ohio. Sometimes the gifts must have been completely unexpected; on one occasion the candidate received a "huge" case of Vermont butter; another time a group gave him a "small" pot of sand, which they claimed "produced oil at a world breaking rate. Likewise this field will produce votes for McKinley." No matter how weird the gift, McKinley always reacted kindly. Presented with the pot of sand, he reportedly "responded fittingly." The gift itself was one thing, but a gracious response to all those willing to bring a present projected the kind of image that Republicans desired. McKinley even wooed the press by sharing one gift with them, passing "generous slices" of a fifty-five-pound watermelon, presented to him with a ribbon of old gold tied around it, to several newspapermen, who thought the treat tasted "luscious."[43]

Campaign managers seemed to invite just about every group they could to Canton, their Republican Mecca, in 1896. According to Robert Wiebe, that year saw the culmination of a decadelong process in which such "island communities" were being contaminated by the forces of industrialization, urbanization, and corporatization. Republican leaders invited groups that tried to protect the community and its members, including labor unions. They even brought in groups that some perceived as threats to these "island communities," such as African Americans, naturalized Italian and Bohemian immigrants, and other ethnic groups. Additionally, groups that spread stories about contamination in communities, such as Prohibitionists, were also invited to visit their candidate and his town. Despite the fact that many "island communities" felt under siege by unwanted outside influences in the summer of 1896, Canton showed the country that these places could still accommodate many different outside forces and groups.

Historians have illuminated the positive aspects of the summer of 1896. But McKinley's organizers also faced a variety of problems in bringing so many people to the small Ohio town. Problems included trouble with the complex train system, organizational difficulties with the processions, overcrowding in the streets and on the candidate's lawn, unvetted moments, public debauchery, and crimes such as pickpocketing and fighting. Yet there were no massive fights between Republican and Democratic groups, no murders, and no major assaults. The *Canton Repository* nevertheless reported a good deal of crime that summer, while some regional organs in Cleveland and Indianapolis reported a small portion of the bad news, and most major news organs in New York and Chicago carried little or nothing about such problems. This careful handling of the news coverage allowed Republican editors and organizers to promote the kind of message they wanted: one rooted in family, safety, prosperity, and happiness surrounding a calm, competent, and consistent candidate.

The front porch campaign probably caused mixed feelings among locals. The owner of a burglarized home or business probably disliked it. But a successful business owner or a resident who enjoyed the commotion must have found the campaign season exhilarating. The average homeowner was probably nervous when going to a parade. While there is no evidence of any "neighborhood watch" programs organized and implemented, neighbors surely looked out for each other's property just as fellow business owners looked out for one another. Most likely, many locals looked at the visiting processions through Canton with an air of skepticism. As early as four days into the campaign, the *Indianapolis Sun* reported that some residents were "already tiring" of the "continuous reception business." In October the *Cleveland Plain Dealer* noted, "modern Cantonians are becoming familiar with delegations and bands playing this fall, and their pampered tastes have been so indulged that they have become extremely critical in regard to both." The sheet opined that in July every resident would come out to see one drum corps and a ward club with "awe and wonder. But the Cantonian has changed since then. He would not go out and meet the world but the world has come to him and the Cantonian of today is as cosmopolitan as the modest squatter who dwelt on the banks of Lake Michigan when the World's Fair moved in next to him." A week later they seemed bored by the incessant visitors: "The citizens here are completely tired out. . . . Hotels and restaurant keepers and their employees were completely exhausted."[44]

While some of the locals may have grown tired of the campaign, it worked. McKinley won 7,105,144 popular votes and 271 electoral votes to Bryan's 6,307,897 and 176. In the eyes of his supporters, the Republican's series of seemingly flawless efforts in 1896 fully legitimized front porch campaigning, while his opponent undertook the most intense, elongated stumping tour in US political history and lost. In late August the *Canton Repository* reprinted articles from newspapers around the country favorably comparing McKinley's style with that of Bryan. The *Milwaukee Evening Wisconsin* stated that the Republican decided to "attend political conventions pending the campaign, in order to address the audience there assembled," without using the term "front-porch campaigning." It declared that the process was "in consonance with the best traditions of the republic," going on to state, "we are gratified that Major McKinley has put his foot upon a practice which in these later years has begun to be prevalent." They were happy that the "noble" candidate had engaged in a practice that "best accords with the dignity of a republic." While Bryan believed in the "stumping doctrine," which he pursued "with the zest of a school-boy," the *Syracuse Post* surmised that for McKinley, "his platform is his front porch: his audience is the world. That beats the tailboard of a railroad train, saves the strength of the candidate and insures him an audience every time." The *Post* noted the importance of the press in helping spread the Ohioan's messages: "His words are flashed across the country and every speech from the front porch of the modest home in Canton is soon the possession of every reading citizen." The *San Francisco Call* also compared McKinley's talks favorably to those made by his opponent: "Mr. Bryan talks flippantly about grave questions, and they see him parade himself as a boy with his first pair of red-top boots would. . . . When McKinley talks the people go to their homes to think. . . . When they leave Mr. McKinley they think of patriotism and prosperity, and when they leave Mr. Bryan they wonder what he is trying to do with the country."[45] Newspapers from across the country not only liked McKinley's talks more than those of Bryan but also thought that front porch campaigning was now consistent with good Republican principles. While McKinley had defeated Bryan, likewise the front porch had defeated the stump.

CHAPTER 4

Between Canton and Marion

The Shady Stump Outshines the
Comfortable Front Porch

The 1908 presidential campaign was the first to see both major-party candidates stump. William Jennings Bryan took to the road for the third time as the Democratic nominee, so he had plenty of experience. The Republican candidate, William Taft, had never run for any political office. Taft decided to stump so that he would not appear disinterested juxtaposed against the always-zealous Bryan. Maybe the most fascinating stop made by the "Taft Special" train was in Fargo, North Dakota. Folks from as far as 450 miles away came to see the candidate. A torchlight procession accompanied Taft through town on his way to a local fort, where a tremendous barbeque was planned. Fourteen bands provided music, and a squad of mounted cowboys accompanied the parade with "their characteristic yells." The *New York Times* described the scene as "picturesque." More to the point, the *Fargo Daily News* posited that the parade was "completely disorganized by the surging meaningless crowd" but admitted that "the demonstration [was] unprecedented in the history of the campaign so far. . . . It is the greatest crowd that has gathered at one time to hear and see Taft, with the possible exceptions of Des Moines and the Twin Cities." Coordinators in Fargo also planned an elaborate meal for the candidate and his followers, serving up twenty mules and ten steers at the barbeque. Two large black bears from Montana were brought in as well. Speeches were made in a cleared area in the woods "in a natural amphitheatre." Log fires and large torches set up around the audience created "a weird light and smoke effect" over them. Taft joked about putting the Democratic Party into the White House, to which a "somewhat elderly" woman yelled, "We don't want to try it." Taft responded: "I hope not, Madam. I have no doubt that you are the heart of a family of sturdy men, whom you control, and I rely on such intelligent ladies as you to carry out your views."[1]

Debate in the press over the fate of the bears at the barbeque illuminated the weight of Theodore Roosevelt's symbolism over the campaign. Famously, the president loved to hunt big game, especially aggressive animals such as bears. In 1903 he traveled to Mississippi, where some locals tied a bear to a tree for him to shoot; however, Roosevelt insisted on hunting the animal. Once this story circulated, the president was given the nickname "Teddy." The *New York Times* claimed that the bears in Fargo were originally going to be part of the meal, having been trapped for some time and fattened with nuts for the occasion. But the locals decided to spare them "because of the sentiment that it would never do to have the candidate eat up the 'real Teddy bear,' as they were designated by a large sign over them." The *Times* claimed that the animals were chained to a table near Taft as he ate. The *Cincinnati Enquirer* and the *Chattanooga Daily Times* backed the story and added that a banner hung over the bears, "We are real teddies." In a completely different report, the *New York Herald* wrote that the animals "were roasted on great spits in the open air" and that Taft "ate the bear meat with as much gusto as any of the thousands of enthusiastics" indulging in free food.[2] The conflicting media stories highlighted a quagmire that Republicans faced while selling Taft: how to properly link him to Roosevelt as a reformer but make him his own man.[3] Maybe more than any other example on the campaign trail, the presence of the bears at the dinner demonstrated the Republican organizers' propensity for effective, spectacle politics.

Stump speaking for the presidency had come a long way since Bryan popularized the technique in 1896. In 1900 Democrat Bryan and Republican vice presidential candidate Roosevelt gave over one thousand stump speeches. In 1908 the presidential candidates dueled each other from the stump for the first time. Four years later the country saw four candidates go on tour, including the sitting president for the first time. What was considered almost taboo in the 1850s, 1860s, and 1870s was becoming commonplace during the early portion of the twentieth century. The front porch technique was abandoned by Taft, Roosevelt, and Bryan as well as Woodrow Wilson later.

While stump speaking rose in popularity, nearly a quarter of a century elapsed between McKinley's sweeping use of the front porch campaign in

Canton in 1896 and Warren Harding's front porch efforts in 1920 in Marion, Ohio. The technique never failed a Republican presidential candidate, so why did they stop using it in the early twentieth century? The answer, in short, proved to be the charasmatic, bold personalities of Bryan and Roosevelt. They were so good at it, and did it so often, that stump speaking became commonplace in the American political mentality by the end of 1912. Gil Troy has also written that as generations changed, people became more accepting of stumping by a presidential candidate as they became less worried about a strong chief executive. The generation of "lingering republicans" born before 1810 wanted to uphold the Founding Fathers' wishes that the office sought the man. Born between 1810 and 1850, a generation of "emerging liberal democrats" accepted a more active nominee—but only to a degree because stumping candidates ran into a lot of trouble and electoral failures between 1852 and 1896. After 1850 a generation of "imperial democrats" wanted an expansive democracy and were much less nervous than their fathers and grandfathers about executive usurpation. Additionally, the front porch campaign rose and fell swiftly because "by 1904 the tactic was suspect. . . . Devised to accommodate the people the front-porch campaign was now deemed a way to hide from them. The shift stemmed from the rise of stumping and the transformation of politics from street theatre to newspaper fare. . . . By 1904 . . . , [r]ather than seek out the nominee, the people wanted the nominee to seek them out."[4] The ubiquity of newspapers helped create an atmosphere in which citizens were increasingly used to everything coming to them, including the news and the candidates themselves. In addition, another important political trend was the growing Progressive movement, which stressed an active government coming down to the local level to help people suffering from the effects of industrialization and urbanization. It made sense that voters experiencing a more active government would expect more active candidates. Suddenly it seemed that aggressive interest for the executive office was in vogue, and any form of disinterestedness was a potential death knell for a candidate.

In 1900 McKinley was in the White House figuring out what to do in the Philippines while his vice presidential candidate, the war hero Roosevelt, actively stumped for him. McKinley did not think that the front porch of the Executive Mansion would be an appropriate place to campaign: "the proprieties demand that the President should refrain from making a political canvass on his own behalf." By 1900 the country had been out of the depression for three years, and many of McKinley's promises from the previous election had come true. By staying quiet, he elevated his level of dignity as an already successful sitting chief magistrate. As Hanna said when the campaign started, "There is only one issue in this campaign, and that is, let well enough alone." McKinley did go on a speaking tour of the Midwest in 1899 in anticipation of the upcoming election, but after the two-week, eighty-speech trip, he declined all other speaking engagements. Bryan ran again in a rare presidential rematch election and gave 546 speeches to nearly 2.5 million people, some of whom were women or children who could not vote. While Republicans were at first nervous to send Roosevelt out in 1900, they eventually caved in. Neither he nor the party could resist the temptation to use his bold, brash personality, which may have been more suited for passionate stump speaking than any presidential candidate ever, including the silver-tongued Bryan. Roosevelt gave 673 speeches to an estimated 3 million voters. The year 1900 proved to be a watershed for stump speaking as the two candidates combined to give more electioneering speeches (1,219) from the stump, the rear platform, or the front porch than any pair of candidates in the nineteenth century. While there was some lingering criticism of Roosevelt's activity in the press, Republicans legitimized his style by publicly bragging about the number of miles he traveled, the amount of hands he shook, the number of speeches he made, and even the railroad systems that he used. McKinley allowed his running mate to upstage him and profited from what was considered taboo by winning the contest. As Troy has written, Bryan and Roosevelt "helped bury a century-long tradition of candidate passivity."[5] While educational campaigning had been in vogue for a little over a decade, these two personalities naturally put the spotlight back on spectacle politics.

Roosevelt's hypermasculine attitude not only helped transform what was acceptable for presidential candidates to do when aggressively seeking the office but also reaffirmed the traditional gender roles challenged by some women who had participated in the front porch campaigns. Roosevelt combined old Democratic themes about the importance of masculinity, harping on the importance of projecting strength in all aspects of life, with middle-class themes highlighting the importance of respectability, especially when he declared that "better men" could solve America's urban issues. He embodied the fears that many middle-class Democrats and Republicans shared about the ubiquity of lower-class behaviors rooted in alcohol consumption, hooliganism, fighting, and other forms of ruffianism that sometimes permeated political contests and urban areas. Republican campaign managers during the Progressive Era were most likely aware that these exact behaviors had, at times, hampered the effectiveness of front porch campaigns in Canton and Indianapolis. Roosevelt also popularized horseback riding, football, boxing, tennis, and outdoor hiking as great ways for men to improve their health and masculinity. Newspapers loved depicting the vice presidential candidate as a Rough Rider, hunter, scout, cowboy, and horseman.

Roosevelt forcefully asserted his opinions on gender roles from the stump and in essays published for public consumption. He told his male listeners that projecting weakness was their greatest sin, that their most important duty as citizens was to protect their personal homes and their national home. He declared that it was an American male's duty to "sow their seed" and have families of their own. For Roosevelt, an American women's primary job was to have at least four children. He told an audience in Chicago in 1899 that the maintenance of these rigid gendered roles was the key to having a strong country, or else the United States would "tremble on the brink of doom." His gendered attitudes not only helped popularize energetic traveling and forceful stumping over a more laidback front porch attempt but also set back women who wanted to participate in national politics. During Gilded Age front porch campaigns, women were integral to the image that the candidates were putting forth for the electorate. They appeared with their wives on their porches while women zealously marched in the processions to their homes—making them centerpieces of the campaigns. During the election of 1900, Bryan and Roosevelt spoke without their wives onstage and without female-dominated processions infusing the headlines describing their campaigns. As Rebecca Edwards has noted, after 1896, women's special role became motherhood.[6] The suffrage movement and women's political participation in general declined during the first decade of the twentieth century.

After Roosevelt received the Republican nomination for the presidency in 1904, he "was uncharacteristically passive, unusually silent," as the tradition of the incumbent in the White House avoiding electioneering even neutralized him. His opponent, New York Court of Appeals chief justice Alton Parker, at first refused to campaign because he thought stumping lacked dignity. Used to quiet law rooms and courthouses, Parker's personality was not really suited for the stump, the front porch, or the rear platform. He actually started planning a front porch campaign at Rosemount—his Hudson River estate in Esopus, New York—but when photographers started invading his hometown and interjecting into his daily life, the Democratic candidate abandoned the plan. Of this, Parker stated, "I reserve the right to put my hands in my pockets . . . without being everlastingly afraid that I shall be snapped by some fellow with a camera." The chief justice also wanted to avoid stumping, but by September, when his campaign seemed to be waning, he could no longer ignore its importance, giving public speeches in New York, New Jersey, and Connecticut. By this time, stump speaking was gaining esteem as a campaign tool. The *Review of Reviews* posited that voters "wanted to see, hear, and know the man, not the rhetorician or debater." The *Saint Louis Dispatch* argued that Parker awoke to the fact that he needed to be heard and now "A Real Campaign," as one headline declared, had begun. The stump was quickly becoming more legitimate than the front porch. The *New York Press* released a cartoon in late July in which Uncle Sam asked Parker, "Why don't you come out on the platform, Alton?" Parker snickered, "Thanks, I prefer the front-porch." The caption underneath the picture flatly stated, "IT'S SAFER!"[7] Roosevelt won the election in a landslide.

In the next three election cycles, the trend toward stumping and male-dominated politics continued. In 1908 Roosevelt's handpicked successor, Taft, did not want to campaign. His opponent, Bryan again, initially claimed that he would not engage in active campaigning but by mid-September found himself stumping, explaining to a crowd in Buffalo, "I am endeavoring to meet the exactions of the campaign." In addition to Bryan, a third-party candidate, Socialist Eugene Debs, campaigned from the back of a train. Taft may have been comfortable front porch campaigning in his hometown of Cincinnati, but legislation had banned railway passes to political rallies and not too many people desired to pay between two and twenty dollars to travel. One paper wrote that the Republican would gain a much clearer picture as to what the American people wanted by actually visiting with them face-to-face. Taft also weighed three hundred pounds and enjoyed playing golf, both characteristics that some considered indicative of a lazy lifestyle. This perception could not possibly assist any presidential candidate, much less one coming after the energetic Roosevelt. Those characteristics combined with a front porch campaign could also be potentially disastrous in the court of public opinion. Taft eventually decided to engage in an 18,000-mile tour in which he gave four hundred speeches. The *New York Times* surmised: "It is not undignified, it is not improper. The people want to see and listen to the men asking their votes." Taft went to states such as Wyoming, Colorado, Minnesota, North and South Dakota, Kansas, and Iowa before traveling south to Tennessee and North Carolina, then north to New York and Connecticut. He exercised witty repartee with both men and women—and made sure to shake all the hands he could. The former judge also connected well with workers throughout the Midwest. Bryan and Taft even encountered each other in Chicago and spoke privately at a dinner before each giving a nonpartisan speech to those assembled. Later, while Bryan was talking up north, Taft's train chugged past him. The Boy Orator smiled and waved at the train, while the Republican's campaigners threw out Taft buttons and campaign literature to bedazzled onlookers. Bryan grinned at the news that his opponent was stumping, stating: "Republican papers . . . said it was demagogic to run around the country hunting for votes. Now it is eminently proper since Mr. Taft is going to do it. My greatest sin is to made virtue by imitation." The contest was the first in which both major-party candidates stumped. As Troy has pointed out, for a presidential candidate by 1908, "passivity was dangerous. . . . Ambition was no longer a dirty word, and was in fact required. Neither Taft nor Bryan wanted to stump in 1908—but they had no choice."[8] It seemed that running from the front porch was becoming antiquated quickly because being *somewhat* interested in the presidency was no longer enough for voters.

While Bryan, Roosevelt, and Taft popularized stump speaking between 1896 and 1908, the drama that the election of 1912 produced stirred criticism of the newly popularized technique. Four candidates actively sought office that year: President Taft, Woodrow Wilson for the Democrats, Debs for the Socialists, and Roosevelt for the Progressive Party. Taft had not handled the presidency to Roosevelt's liking, and the former president decided to challenge his successor for the Republican nomination. There were now twelve direct primaries for the nomination, so voters could directly choose delegates for their favorite man. Both Roosevelt and Taft stumped, eventually calling each other names like "fathead," "egotist," and "puzzlewit." Taft was "humiliated" by the fact that he was the "first one [sitting president] that has had to depart from the tradition that keeps the President at home during political controversies."[9] Following his defeat of Roosevelt at the Republican convention, Taft stopped publicly campaigning, while Roosevelt continued. There was an assassination attempt on the Bull Moose candidate in mid-October; he survived the shot and gave a campaign speech while bleeding lightly.[10] The *New York Times* labeled the dueling stumping for the nomination a "spectacle . . . [that] should bring a blush of shame to the cheek of every American."[11] This comment on campaign styles demonstrated that the push toward educational campaigns had influenced some observers over the years. To an extent, in 1888 James Clarkson was right when he sensed the growing need for such campaigns. Yet many voters still wanted to see the candidates and "feel" their personalities, showing that the penchant for spectacle politics had not worn off for many.

Like Taft, Wilson also disliked stumping, telling one friend that while he did not mind talking, he did not want to be dragged halfway across the country on a speechmaking tour. Yet Roosevelt's personality managed to pull Wilson to the stump as well. As Troy has stated, "The college professor feared the Rough Rider." Wilson was afraid of the power of Roosevelt's personality, positing that the former president was "a real, vivid person, whom they have seen and shouted themselves hoarse over and voted for, millions strong. I am a vague conjectural personality, more made up of opinions and academic prepossession than of human traits and red corpuscles." Wilson spoke extemporaneously, like Bryan, which made it hard for the press to copy down his statements; nor did he like to attack his opponents. Troy also has pointed out that the Virginian sometimes campaigned against campaigning while he campaigned—even sounding professorial when doing so. In Indiana, Wilson stated: "I have tried discussing the big questions of this campaign from the rear end of a train. It can't be done. They are too big. . . . By the time you get started and begin to explain yourself the train moves on." But over time the Democrat also took to stumping like Taft had, even writing that he knew he had arrived in politics "when an old fellow . . . slapped me on the back and shouted: 'Doc, you're alright; give it to 'em.'" Like Taft, Wilson eventually warmed up to touring, and it helped him win the election. Also like Taft, he had been motivated to the stump by the fierce personality of Roosevelt. The process transformed Wilson from being an austere professor to a relatively folksy candidate. After the contest was over, the Democratic Party chairman exclaimed, "We won in 1912 because the personality of Woodrow Wilson had captured the country."[12] Now two candidates in a row had won the presidency from the stump.

With the outbreak of the Great War in August 1914, Wilson had to deal with a myriad of issues that he did not have to discuss two years previous. He campaigned on the slogan "He Kept Us out of War" in 1916 because he had successfully done so up to that point while preparing for the worst. He had also pushed a series of Progressive legislation through Congress. Wilson claimed that the exigencies of the executive office did not allow for time to stump. His record would stand for itself, although he did assure his campaign manager that his "whole heart" was in the reelection bid. As Troy has written, "The President was too busy saving the world and reforming the nation to campaign actively."[13]

The Republicans nominated Supreme Court justice Charles Hughes. In 1912 Hughes flatly stated, "A man on the Supreme Bench who would run for public office is neither fit for the office he holds nor for the one to which he aspires." Four years later he resigned from the court to accept the Republican nomination. Hughes believed in the traditional adage that the nomination for the presidency should never be sought nor refused, so when the party sought him out, he could not decline. He needed to project a strong image in 1916 because his party was divided over the war and Progressivism. The Republican candidate decided to mount an energetic tour: "When I was a judge I was 100 per cent Judge. When I am a candidate for office I am 100 per cent a candidate."[14]

Hughes's tour started with a head of steam, but he wound up encountering multiple problems on the road that ultimately hurt his candidacy and contributed to his loss. Accompanied by his pretty wife, the former justice warmed up to the folks that he visited fairly quickly. He attended a baseball game and met Ty Cobb. The candidate visited nine cities in Maine right before they held their September congressional elections; the Republican vote increased in those cities 45 percent, while it increased in all other areas of the state by 24 percent. One local observer attributed the tide of Republican popularity there to the simple "presence" of Hughes. But the candidate's extemporaneous speaking style often left him at odds with the press because they could not reproduce his exact words—the same problem as with Bryan in 1896 and Wilson in 1912. Hughes also formed the habit of attacking the president, after which the crowds began to reflect a distinct lack of energy: "People wondered how this sober Dr. Jekyll had become a demagogic Mr. Hyde," as Troy has put it. Hughes even made the mistake of personally visiting with Jeremiah O'Leary, the president of a group of German Americans and Irish Americans opposed to the United Kingdom and the other Allied powers. When O'Leary asked Wilson to clarify his position on the war, the president replied with a telegram stating pointedly: "I would feel deeply mortified to have you or anybody like you vote for me. Since you have access to many disloyal Americans and I have not, I will ask you to convey this message to them." Probably most importantly, when Hughes traveled to California, his "Old Guard" Republicans failed to arrange a visit for him with the popular Progressive Republican Hiram Johnson, who was then running for a US Senate seat. Hughes even stayed in the same hotel as Johnson one night, but his handlers did not arrange for a meeting and press coverage. As Troy has pointed out, this oversight became a snub.[15] Hughes lost California that year. The former justice started his tour feeling a little like Roosevelt, but he wound up looking like Blaine in 1884.

Despite being too busy trying to save the world, Wilson also managed to go on a speaking tour late in the campaign. The president insisted that he was participating in no such political activity, claiming from the back of the train as it stopped in different towns, "I am not making a speechmaking campaign." But Wilson once again managed to campaign against campaigning while he campaigned.[16] The former professor managed to pull off such a feat twice in a row, though he barely defeated Hughes in the Electoral College.

Between Canton in 1896 and Marion in 1920, stump speaking clearly usurped front porch campaigning as the popular method of running for the presidency. The personalities of Bryan and Roosevelt accounted tremendously for this surge. Bryan wanted to act differently than other Gilded Age candidates, so his front porch was not an option. Roosevelt's personality and image made him perfect for touring; he would have snickered at homebound campaigning and probably considered it emasculating. These two personalities, along with the expansion of newspapers and the federal government during the Progressive Era, all combined to contribute to the popularity of active campaigning for the presidency. If the local store could provide a newspaper in one's hometown, and an enlarged federal government could provide more services on the local level, then it logically followed that voters would expect the candidates to visit them—even if it was just for a few moments. Touring made it possible for candidates to combine spectacle, educational, and advertising politics while seeming appropriately interested in the office; front porch campaigning came off as too disinterested in an era when disinterestedness had to go up against the public perceptions and feelings that Roosevelt and Bryan evoked in the electorate.

While Roosevelt and Bryan are always highlighted in history books and lectures, probably the most interesting candidates of this age were Wilson and Taft. Presidential candidates Roosevelt and Bryan vociferously stumped in a total of four elections and lost all of them. They brought extremely high skill sets to each contest, but that did not translate into victory. While neither Taft nor Wilson were excited to tour, they won three of the four elections in which they did—Wilson handing Taft his only loss in 1912. While Taft became the first incumbent president to tour in 1912, Wilson became the first president to stump and retain the office four years later. Both men transformed their image while they campaigned: Taft went from a seemingly isolated judge and secretary of war to a relatively energetic, affable candidate; Wilson went from a stuffy professor to a folksy, down-to-earth kind of guy. Other men, such as Parker and Hughes, were wilted by the experience. Bryan and Roosevelt may have made stumping trendy, but Taft and Wilson used the technique to change their public images and win elections. Once considered taboo, stumping for the presidency was now in vogue.

CHAPTER 5

Phonographs, Friendly Reporters, and the Final Front Porch Campaign

The Merchandizing of Warren Harding in 1920

In August 1920 Republican candidate Warren Harding conducted a shrewdly staged front porch campaign event from his home in Marion, Ohio. He hosted a group of two hundred reporters to give them a talk about a variety of subjects, including the future of the newspaper industry. Making them feel a little extra important was a smart move; these were the folks who were reporting the events that he was creating from his front porch to reading audiences around the country. The candidate outlined several problems facing the business, including the rising costs of equipping a newspaper plant. He also surmised that a general lack of timber was causing the cost of paper to go up for many outlets. Harding suggested creating a forest-development policy that would make the United States self-reliant on timber. He opined: "Forest conservation is a necessary accompaniment to printing expansion, and a matter of common concern to all people. Three/Fifths of our original timber is gone and 80,000,000 acres of land exist for planting new trees to ensure paper production for newspaper outlets." Harding not only endeared himself to the editors in his audience, but he also must have caught the ear of many other editors around the country when they heard about his concerns. After the talk Harding and his wife, Florence, shook hands with all of the reporters as well as their wives and children. The candidate came off personably as he interacted with some of his former colleagues: "Hi Elmer," he shouted to one, and "How's the Sentinel, Sam?" to another. The *New York Tribune* noted, "He knew them all, had known their fathers, and Mrs. Harding's acquaintance among them was just as complete." Two weeks later Gifford Pinchot, Teddy Roosevelt's original pick as chief of the US Forest Service, endorsed Harding's conservation plan.[1]

The timing of the candidate's message was almost as strategic as the content of his talk. The friendly get-together between Harding and the press took place in the middle of August—three weeks after he started campaigning. These very same reporters would continue to give the Republican's other staged events friendly coverage for the next two months before the election. In 1920 Harding made members of the press feel like they were a part of his own family. His relationship with them may have been better than any other previous nominee. Their coverage of the parades to Harding's house and the gatherings for his speeches from his front porch made the Republican candidate a hit with the American public.

The strategy worked—Harding won over 60.3 percent of the popular vote and achieved a landslide in the Electoral College over Democrat James Cox. His front porch campaign in Marion from July 31 through October 18 helped him showcase his folksy personality, his "common man" background, his interests, and his family. During his talks, Harding shared his views on the League of Nations, the need for tighter immigration laws and higher tariff schedules, and his support for trade unionism and collective bargaining, African American rights, women voting nationally for the first time, farmers, conservation, and maintaining an active government as a Republican leader. In September and October several "Super Days" were organized for specific groups, such as African Americans, women, and naturalized voters, to visit.[2] Harding offered up platitudes and lip service to these constituencies, just like his front porch predecessors. Republican National Committee chairman Will Hays and famous advertising executive Albert D. Lasker also put together the first modern advertising campaign for a presidential candidate. Lasker put Harding's photogenic face on a number of journals and magazines as well as billboards, posters, and the early movie screen to sell his candidacy throughout the country. Twice a week he sent out "photographic bulletins" of Harding and his wife so the public could consume them and remember the folksy candidate in a homebound, "normal" setting.[3] As a result of this last front porch campaign, Harding's popular win was larger than three of Franklin Roosevelt's four landslides.

Historians have come up with several reasons for Harding's electoral success. His personality, his campaigners' ability to market his all-American persona, and the spirit of community and "civic boosterism" that pervaded Marion throughout the summer of 1920 were certainly all contributing factors to his victory.[4] Like his predecessors, Harding staged a series of events designed to reach a larger audience through newspapers. His campaign managers did not hide the fact that these were major staged events by giving them particular labels to brand them even more effectively, including "Colored Voters Day," "Women Voters Day," and "First-Time Voters Day." Marion was a town well positioned to be another midwestern "island community" that harkened back to the less complicated days before the Great War, heavy industrialization, and the resulting shift from rural- to urban-oriented values. In front of this effective backdrop, Harding delivered a message of "America First" through isolation from the world community in foreign affairs and a mixture of reforms at home to help working-class and middle-class families. He employed the words "protection," "patriotism," "family," and "home" the same way that McKinley had. Republican managers shrewdly advertised and sold a highly polished version of Harding as a nice, patriotic, down-to-earth family man through newspapers, phonographs, the radio, and movies. This image was juxtaposed next to his Democratic opponent, James Cox, a traveling divorced man going on "one night stands" when he visited a town for a few moments, spoke, and then rode on to the next town. Harding's carefully orchestrated love affair with the press, and his campaigners' ability to merchandize him as a patriot and family man who wanted to put the United States first, propelled the candidate to an overwhelming victory.

Campaign manager Harry Daugherty played the pivotal role in motivating Harding to run for the presidency and also in securing support for his nomination from other Republican delegates. Born thirty-five miles southwest of Columbus, Ohio, at the Washington County House, Daugherty (like Mark Hanna) managed to find himself in trouble as a youth. He and his brother tapped telegraph wires to pick up advance notices on horse-racing results. Later Daugherty vacillated between being a lawyer and trying to climb the Ohio political ladder. One analyst from Columbus at the time stated that the only election that he could win would be the "Order of the Tin Can." A year after he vacated the position of Ohio's lieutenant governor in 1907, Harding wrote: "The amiable and talented Mr. Daugherty shuddering about bossism is a spectacle to amuse all of Ohio. We like Daugherty, but he held a high seat in the bossing procession, when there was Hanna absolutism in this state and never said a word." Five years later the complicated campaign of 1912 politically allied the editor and the operative because they both supported

Taft over Roosevelt for the Republican nomination. Both men stuck together as pro-Taft delegates-at-large at the Republican convention at which they weathered the Roosevelt storm. Following the general election, Daugherty wrote to Harding that he felt the campaign had brought them closer together and that in the future they would stay "together through thick and thin." Internal party strife estranged the two in 1918—by which time Harding was a US senator from Ohio—but Roosevelt's death a year later brought them together again. In November 1919 Harding wrote to a friend, "I have always felt I could depend on Daugherty, though he did give me a little annoyance during the trying period we passed through last winter." As 1920 approached, Harding expressed ambivalence about running for president, but Daugherty helped talk him into it. The senator asked him, "Am I a big enough man for the race?" Daugherty demonstrated his political introspection with his response: "Don't make me laugh! The day of giants in the Presidential chair is passed. Our so-called Great Presidents were all made by the conditions of war under which they administered the office. Greatness in the presidential chair is largely an illusion of the people."[5]

For the first six months of the campaign year, it appeared that the Republican Party was just as ambivalent about picking a candidate for the presidency as Harding was about running. The party actually had nine possible nominees throughout the early part of the year: Spanish-American War general Leonard Wood, California senator Hiram Johnson, Illinois governor Frank Lowden, Massachusetts governor Calvin Coolidge, Kansas governor Henry Allen, Columbia University president Nicholas Butler, Pennsylvania governor William C. Sproul, Great War general John Pershing, and Senator Harding. Smaller movements for Allen, Butler, and Sproul died down relatively quickly. Pershing decisively lost the Nebraska primary, which effectively eliminated him from the field. After gaining national acclaim for his active role in breaking up the Boston Police Strike in September 1919, Coolidge started to gain national traction, but in January 1920 he publicly claimed that he was not in contention for the race because he did not have enough money. Going into the Republican convention in June 1920, then, Wood, Johnson, Lowden, and Harding were the four serious contenders for the nomination.[6]

The four men had run against each other in a series of twenty primaries. The contests complicated rather than clarified the race due to the several serious contenders as well as vague state laws that often did not bind delegates to vote for the candidate who won the popular vote. Wood spent $1,773,000 on the primaries and gained 124 delegates, while Johnson received 965,000 popular votes, the most of any candidate, but secured only 112 delegates. Lowden spent $415,000 and had 72 delegates to show for it, while Harding came in fourth with a paltry 39 delegates. Wood and Johnson had big personalities that some party leaders liked but that put off others. Wood's extravagant spending turned off a lot of leaders, while Johnson's alleged "irreconcilability" toward the League of Nations damaged him. Apparently, Lowden "could get along with men of almost every stripe," and there were charges that he had bought delegates in Missouri. Harding only ran in two primaries, failing to capture all of the delegates in his home state and coming in fourth in neighboring Indiana. Daugherty worked endlessly to help secure more delegate support for him. Although the Ohio senator did poorly in the primaries he contested, Daugherty still managed to meet with almost 75 percent of the delegates in all twenty states and sought their support for Harding as their second- or third-place choices, crucial in the coming convention. When the Republican delegates did gather in Chicago, they saw ten ballots taken. On the first one, Wood led with 287.5 delegates, with Harding's 65.5 placing him fifth. By the ninth ballot, Harding had 374.5 delegates and led; on the tenth ballot the party made him their unanimous choice; later they selected Coolidge as his running mate. The change in Harding's position can be attributed to his affable personality, his moderate positions, and his reputation as a staunch party man. After the first day of balloting, Republican leaders, including Chairman Hays and Henry Cabot Lodge, held a series of late-night meetings with party insiders in a "smoke-filled room" at the Blackstone Hotel and decided that Harding would be the best and most effective compromise candidate. They accurately predicted that the Democratic Party would nominate Cox, who also hailed from Ohio. Party leaders felt not only that Harding could compete with Cox for that key swing state's electoral votes more effectively than any other candidate but also that they could control him once he attained the executive office.[7] In 1919 Harding was a little-known senator from Ohio. Suddenly, in June 1920, he was the Republican nominee for the presidency.

Harding was born in 1865 in Blooming Grove, Ohio. At the age of ten, his father purchased a newspaper called the *Argus,* which allowed his son to become familiar with the print business. Harding attended Ohio Central College, where he continued to work in the newspaper business with the *Union Register* in Mount Gilead. He also became an accomplished orator while in college and graduated in 1882 while only seventeen. After he finished school, Harding purchased the *Marion Star* with a partner and became its full owner in 1886. He turned the paper into a pro-Republican sheet, which put him at odds with many Marion leaders as well as the town's other paper, the pro-Democratic *Marion Independent*. Five years later the controversial newspaperman married Florence Kling, who had been previously married and whose father was the editor of the *Independent*. Florence played a large role in motivating Harding to keep running for political offices and liked being a major part of his decision-making entourage. She also helped turn the *Star* into a profitable business. By 1893 it had overtaken the *Independent* as Marion's most popular paper. Six years later Harding won a seat in the Ohio State Senate. Shortly after that victory he met Daugherty, who later commented to a friend that Harding would make a great-looking president. From 1904 to 1906, Harding served as the lieutenant governor of Ohio after a failed bid for the gubernatorial nomination in 1903. Harding finally ran for governor in 1909 and lost. Five years later his inconsistent political career took a turn when he was selected to be a US senator. This was the office that Harding occupied when he won the Republican nomination for the presidency.[8] Following the convention in mid-June, Harding was faced with the same question that Garfield, Harrison, and McKinley had contemplated about the presidential contest: should he stay home, let the office seek him, and appear disinterested; should he hit the road, give campaign speeches, and aggressively seek the office; or should he stay at home and try to strike a balance between disinterest and interest by running a front porch campaign?

A statement that Harding made as the leader of the 1916 Republican convention foreshadowed his decision: he thought that Hughes "would have fared much better had he gone to his summer residence . . . and remained there, and retained the halo about his head which came on his exceptional nomination." While Harding tried to figure out how to create and maintain a halo over his own head, the Republican Party debated whether or not he should stay on his porch or hit the road. Some Ohio party leaders told national-committee members that they did not want to see him stay in Marion, believing that the voters in Ohio were already acquainted with the former editor and that he needed more public exposure in the West and other states in the Midwest. The committee favored a "swing around the circle" for their candidate rather than "the passive campaign that has been advocated in some quarters." (The title above the newspaper article reporting this read, "OHIO DOES NOT WANT HARDING TO SIT ON PORCH.") Other Republican leaders seemed to agree with the committee members on the subject—when the press asked Wood whether or not Harding should go on tour, he gave an insightful answer: "I think there is a big difference between primary and general campaigns. In the primary a man would not get far by issuing a few statements. There are too many men in the field. The people want to see the candidates. They will not read all the speeches. But where the nominee is picked it is different." Democratic vice presidential candidate Franklin Roosevelt agreed with Wood for different reasons: "The Democrats will drive Senator Harding from his front porch in Marion and force him to take the stump at an early date in the campaign."[9]

Harding's managers knew that they would have to somehow gin up attention and excitement for the campaign to overcome an initially lukewarm, if not negative, response to the nomination. In early July Elizabeth Reid had written to one of Harding's leading campaign strategists: "A good many hope for the best, but there is no enthusiasm at all. There seems instead to be a state of apathy. How are we going to get people interested enough to work for and to believe in Senator Harding? He is not well-known to the people and his nomination is considered a maneuver of the political, planned last winter by Senators and Congressmen, and carried through. It is thought to have been done because the leaders felt they could more easily influence Senator Harding than any other candidate."[10] Just a few days later, a political onlooker named Burt Cady linked the Ohio Republican's reputation as a party puppet with the need for him to hit the stump.

> I consider it absolutely necessary that Senator Harding take the stump. There is a sentiment, which, of course, is unfair and unjust, that Senator Harding's nomination was brought about by a reactionary and conservative element who are closely aligned with the big interests. It is plain talk that his nomination was agreed upon months before the convention was held and that he was not in reality a dark horse. I know all these statements are absolutely false, but the feeling is abroad and being spread largely by our enemies and it is my judgement that the only way to overcome it is to have Senator Harding take the stump and meet the people and let them see and hear him and be convinced that he is a man well-qualified for the Presidency. It is going to be impossible to take the large vote we need in this state [Michigan] in order to win down to Marion to visit the candidate. I consider this the largest question you have to determine during the campaign.[11]

Eventually, Harding did hit the road, but only after porch campaigning for the majority of the season.

The lavish, negative primary campaigns that the Republican hopefuls ran against each other in the spring also had a big influence on Harding's decision. Many of his advisors then had told him to stay home so that his pursuit of the nomination would seem more dignified than Wood's expensive run. Republican leaders such as Albert Beveridge, Sen. Harry S. New, John Weeks, and Stewart Davison all had suggested a more dignified front porch effort than the "rich man's primaries." Now it seemed that the aggressive techniques used by Bryan and Roosevelt were starting to take a backseat again to the more "dignified" front porch campaign. In a letter to Harding, Ohio political observer Myron Herrick bemoaned the negative nature of the primary contest between Wood and Johnson as well as the one in Ohio between Harding and Wood. Besides the additional room for mudslinging, Herrick also worried about the lavish spending they had promoted: "This, it seems to me, should be the last and final crushing argument against the primaries, for neither Lowden nor Wood spent illegitimately, and we should do all we can to relieve them of the smirch of a money campaign, which, in the eyes of so many people who do not know, has left them in disgrace."[12] In the Gilded Age, "dignified" meant not stumping too much; by 1920, it meant not spending too much money.

The failure of Hughes's tour in 1916 also affected Harding. Albert Shaw wrote to the Ohioan that on his own front porch, "you can afford to be very deliberate, wholly unruffled and exceedingly good tempered." Hughes had become ruffled and shrill from the stump as his tour lagged on. Herrick also explained to Harding that he had almost persuaded Hughes to campaign from his home—the former justice was "very much impressed and came very near making that sort of campaign. Had he done so, the untoward circumstances in California could not have occurred, and he would have been elected." He also recounted how McKinley had stayed on his front porch because it gave him time to think about what he was going to say, it allowed newsmen to accurately report his words to millions, and it helped him maintain his health. Herrick now advised Harding to think of his own health as well as the health of the campaign.[13]

Sen. Walter Edge also weighed in on campaign strategy, writing to Harding that he should "go home to Ohio, remain for a week or two receiving the formal and informal visits that would naturally follow your return, and divide the holiday period in the summer from approximately the first of July to early September in two resort sections of the country, still maintaining the same policy of gladly welcoming delegations and visitors, but having them come to you rather than you going to them." Unlike Herrick, Edge apparently did not think that the lavish spending in the primaries meant much in the court of public opinion by suggesting that the candidate stay at two different resort locations. Edge liked to take credit for giving Harding the idea of remaining in Marion, yet on the same day that he wrote to the candidate, Hays, now the campaign chairman, told the press that Harding would only make a dozen or so speeches across the country and would conduct a "porch campaign." Harding ignored the advice to stay at a resort because he did not want to project the image of a wealthy candidate on vacation during an election season. Along with Hays, Edge, and Herrick, Senator New of Indiana protested against turning Harding into a "whirling dervish" of a candidate, while national-committee member Herbert Parsons warned against "circus" performances because he thought it best to make "full use of the local color of Marion, Ohio."[14]

Harding himself thought that there were several drawbacks to traveling and campaigning: "It develops an unfortunate side of our political activities to have a presidential candidate chasing about the country soliciting support. . . . One cannot be his best in conveying his thoughts to the people whose confidence he desires to enlist." He explained to a *Chicago Tribune* writer that, as an editor in 1897, he had tried to garner an interview with Mark Hanna, who refused. "This shows how a man, travelling, can cross his wires without knowing it, and that's the reason I decided on a front-porch campaign this summer. I wanted to avoid those crossed wires." The candidate also understood that the public needed to hear him speak about Progressivism and international politics: "The country is calling for deliberate utterance, and that is why the front porch appeals so strongly to me." Despite the recent upsurge in stumping for the presidency, the positive prospects of a homebound run in 1920 made it seem attractive again. The Harding camp announced on June 16 that his front porch campaign would begin two weeks later.[15]

Importantly, even when Harding's plans were announced, the *Marion Star* also noted that he would speak in at least six or eight cities, including New York City, Chicago, San Francisco, and Los Angeles. The plan was further evidence that stumping was usurping homebound campaigning. The sheet vaguely promised that the candidate would cover "all the territory it is considered necessary for him to reach personally." While the paper made its audience aware that Harding would be stumping, it still insisted that he was maintaining a distance from a "barnstorming tour," as they characterized those that had "marked the more recent presidential campaigns." The *Star* rationalized that Harding's front porch efforts would be more sincere than whistle-stop tours, or political "one-night stands," which the paper posited were "not in keeping with the dignity of a candidate for the highest office in the land."[16] For the *Star,* Harding could talk from his front porch and still go on limited stumping tours while maintaining his "dignity" as a candidate in the fluid world of presidential-campaign styles.

Other sheets even more fully supported Harding's decision and lauded front porch campaigning in the process. The *Chicago Tribune* opined: "Harding has decided to fight the campaign from his front porch—a wise decision. It is a return to a sound American tradition. It will appeal to home folks and it's home folks who elect presidents, as well for us they do." The paper claimed that the Republican could become cozier with the electorate from his porch: "A man on his front porch is nearer to a hundred and twenty millions of his countrymen than he is on the near platform of a Pullman. A man on his front porch sees farther than he can from an observation car. He talks less but he thinks more." The sheet also surmised that Harding's porch helped him more effectively identify with common men: "He is more eloquent on the porch because he becomes a symbol of the lives of the people, the useful plodding day-to-day life of us all." Finally, the *Tribune* believed that the porch campaign would open up communication between the candidate and the voters: "He is going to do his own thinking and try to know what we are thinking. . . . He is going to watch the neighbors come across the lawn and he is going to listen to what they have to say." Even though the porch technique had not been used by a candidate since 1896, for the *Tribune,* it was still a "sound American tradition."[17]

Newspapers from around the country joined the *Tribune* in backing Harding's candidacy. The *Los Angeles Times* reprinted several newspaper editorials from Portland, Oregon, praising the Republican as soon as he launched his front porch campaign. The editorials all agreed that by bringing Harding into the White House, the end of "one-man rule" in government would be upon America. The papers viewed President Wilson as a dictator and Harding as the purveyor of the Constitution. The Los Angeles paper also reprinted editorials from Salt Lake City, San Francisco, and Kansas City that offered similar praise for the Republican candidate. A day later the *Times* reprinted other positive editorials of Harding's performances from New York City, Pittsburgh, and Philadelphia.[18]

Other onlookers criticized the notion of a front porch campaign. A Pennsylvania sheet quoted that state's senators: "The so called 'front-porch' campaign, systematically carried out, is largely a thing of the past, and that with modern methods of travel, and the desire of the people to meet the nominee, it would be well to tour the country. . . . [Harding] has a winning personality and makes friends wherever he goes. He has that peculiar quality which goes by the name of magnetism, but which may also be described as human sympathy." In this case, criticism levied against porch campaigning was rooted in the positive qualities that Harding had as a candidate. Another analyst criticized the potential logistics of a porch campaign from Marion, writing to one of Harding's campaign managers, "I hope the sentimental value of the front porch campaign will not be entirely lost when Harding speaks a mile and a half from his front porch in a park that is reached by one car-line and a comparatively narrow street."[19]

Although some critics and locals did not support Harding's style, most of the town mobilized upon finding out that they were about to become the new "Republican Mecca." Like folks in Indianapolis and Canton the previous century, Marion residents prepared themselves for the throngs that were coming and the attention that it would generate. Local leaders took the prospect of the campaign to try to improve the city's infrastructure and cleanliness. Marion's leaders had shown an early penchant for being sensitive to public perceptions of the city when dignitaries and other visitors came, but more was now needed. At a city council meeting held just one day after Harding received the nomination, a local attorney suggested enlarging the city's police force and pointed out the need for making important repairs to certain streets in the city and installing more streetlights. Furthermore, the city's streets and alleys needed to remain clean and council members needed to regulate taxicab fares so that drivers would not overcharge visitors. Dr. C. W. Sawyer next explained how the city needed a hospital for visitors who may become suddenly ill or have an accident. Finally, fire chief Thomas McFarland voiced support for the city's "clean-up plan" but detailed some of the trouble encountered with "some of the leading citizens" over sanitation. He declared that 98 percent of the city's population was doing its part, but the police had to ensure that the other 2 percent also lived up to their responsibilities.[20]

While residents prepared for Harding's formal notification day on July 22, they also consulted with McKinley's former organizers. The secretary of the Marion Civic Association, Carroll Huntress, went to Canton to learn what Republicans had done to plan out McKinley's campaign. The *Marion Star* noted, "It is expected that the problems which will confront Marion this summer will parallel those which Canton was called upon to solve during the summer of 1896 and an ultimate understanding of what was done there is considered invaluable." The ties between the McKinley campaign and Harding's were cemented on July 19, when the flagpole from the late president's front yard was "deposited . . . carefully" onto Harding's lawn. McKinley's flag itself arrived in Marion on the twenty-second.[21]

As Harding's notification day approached, the Marion Civic Association and the Republican organizing committee went into preparation overdrive. D. R. Crissinger claimed that preparations had been made to feed two meals to 100,000 people, although no one knew how many would actually show up. Thirty special trains were also prepared to transport visitors into town. Harding claimed that although no concerted effort had been made by his supporters to solicit visitors, it still looked like July 22 would be a big occasion; he took this as a sign of renewed interest in the Republican Party. Crissinger further stated: "There will be no profiteering. The civic association has discussed the question of prices with merchants and restaurant keepers and respectable process will prevail. If any irresponsible parties are found charging excessive prices then their places will be closed on the spot."[22]

The *Chicago Tribune* explained that Marion, with its 20,000 residents, was preparing to welcome 50,000 visitors on notification day. Of course, that would be just the beginning of the front porch campaign. The paper pointed out that nearly every home in the city had a picture of Harding hanging in the living room. Decorators from Cincinnati were brought in, and an "old circus man," who had fed crowds in Canton, came to town to "make sure that everyone gets a sandwich and a coffee at least." The sheet claimed that a food "emergency" was occurring, so "bakers, butchers, restaurant men, lodges, churches, and housewives have been called on in the emergency. The bakers have given assurances that they can bake 50,000 loaves of bread a day, with an unlimited supply of buns and doughnuts." A large tent was set up in Garfield Park, where Harding would accept the nomination and people would be fed. Also, a number of hotdog stands would be set up around town that day; a local wienerwurst factory could produce "between five and ten tons" of hotdogs per day. Every housewife in Marion was asked to roast a ham on notification day as well as to bake extra bread and to provide coffee for all of the guests. The town was prepared to park 10,000 cars, and Crissinger claimed that 1,000 rooms in private homes would be available to accommodate overnight visitors.[23] Marion appeared to be ready for its moment in the national spotlight.

While railroad rates and overcrowding served as small hindrances to Harding's campaign, for the most part the staged events went smoothly because he played well with the visiting delegations. As historians have recounted, large groups of war veterans, labor-union members, farmers, editors and publishers, businessmen, Native Americans, African Americans, European immigrants, and women all came to see the candidate. His organizers formed a "visiting delegations" bureau, a "colored" voters department, and departments for women's activities, colleges, labor, and traveling salesmen. The Harding home proved inviting to guests; painted dark green with white trim, its front porch was "handsomely" tiled. In 1899 the original front porch had collapsed under the weight of too many visitors arriving to congratulate Harding for winning a state senate seat. It had been rebuilt to run the entire length of the house, ending "in a large protuberance resembling a bandstand." According to Harding biographer Robert Murray, from his remodeled front porch, Harding was "the picture of American respectability, greeting delegations in his white trousers, blue coat, and sawtooth straw hat." The link between the front porch campaign and the dignity of the candidate was not lost on observers. William Allen White wrote to Harding in October: "Just a word to let you know that you are making a great impression on the American people. You have grown every moment since the day of the nomination. It seems to me that your sincerity, your sense of dignity and your steady thoughts have made themselves felt in the American heart." Another political observer wrote to Harding that while Cox "was campaigning all over the lot, in a sweat, in his mental shirt sleeves, with his coat, [and] ringing fire alarms," the Republican came off as "a quiet gentlemen who had no beads on his forehead, no dust on his shoes, [and] no red in his eye." According to this observer, such images won and lost campaigns: "They are not produced by accident. They are produced sometimes by the instinct of a man like Harding. The only certain way to produce them is by the conscious art of political strategy." Another commentator thought the public perceived Cox as "a little like a frontier 'bad man' shooting up the meeting," while Harding appeared in "a very orderly and dignified way, with great decorum and ceremony," as one who had intelligently ignored his opponent's challenge to "get off the front porch, and cut out that pink tea—I'm here with the rough stuff."[24]

The front porch campaign also helped Harding's handlers advertise him in a way that no other presidential candidate had ever been. Particularly in 1920, when the mass consumer culture in American society was just forming, his publicists were ahead of the trend as they perfected the art of making their candidate highly consumable for voters. Many of the techniques they employed were made easier, or even possible, because Harding stayed on his porch for the majority of the campaign and did not barnstorm around the country. The Republican committee unleashed Lasker on the public after Harding received the nomination. He then put on an advertising campaign that had never been seen before by creating a series of billboards, photographs, lithographs, movies, posters, buttons, cartoons, banners, and streamers that projected the candidate's handsome and dignified image to millions of male and female voters around the country. The campaign also generated pamphlets on 150 different subjects pertaining to the election, including such titles as *What Republican Women Can Do in the Election Districts* and *Wanted: A New Business Management for the United States.* Lasker made sure to have brochures for African Americans, such as *Why the Negro Should Vote for a Republican President* and another simply titled *Lynching.* Republicans even experimented with using hot-air balloons and parachutes to project images of their man. In order to help fine-tune the advertising process in print, Chairman Hays produced an instructional pamphlet titled *Suggestions for Public Utterances and Interviews Relative to Harding and Coolidge.* Several of the words and phrases were effective in promoting Harding's front porch campaign, including, "a vote for Harding means a vote for the home" and, "He has fought for and voted to protect our children." Other phrases hinted at the dignity of the candidate, such as "simple, plain unassuming" and "a splendid type of clean American manhood." Still others helped reinforce the idea that Harding was a common man: "born poor," "man of the people," and "his employees . . . take their troubles, their joys, and their worries to him." Home, protection of children, family, and dignity were all part of Harding's front porch campaign and the various pitches to sell him around the country. In a letter to Hays, W. H. Hamilton summed up the Republican mantra on electing political candidates by 1920: "Electing a political candidate is almost entirely a matter of publicity, calling for all that is best in the 'art of advertising and selling,' putting the merits of the candidate and his principles before the largest number of people."[25]

Republican managers also started experimenting with new technology, such as the phonograph and movies, to effectively brand their man. On August 5 Harding spoke into a phonograph machine about issues such as liberty, taxation, and the League of Nations so that his voice could be reproduced for millions of voters to hear. One paper described the activity as "one of his odd jobs during the day." The *Chicago Tribune* wrote that now "canned speeches will supplement the front porch." Harding actually gave five speeches for which his only audience was the recording apparatus in front of him. The records produced from these sessions would be distributed by the Republican National Committee "as a means of carrying the front porch campaign into every locality."[26]

Understanding the vital role that the press would play in relaying his words and images to millions, Harding fostered an extreme amount of goodwill with the newspaper editors who visited and stayed in Marion. He also knew how well McKinley had treated newspapermen in 1896. Aware of the reporters' specific deadlines, he made sure to supply them with material that he knew they desired in a timely fashion. Harding answered all questions candidly and without becoming angry, making clear what information should be used and what should be discarded. Robert McCoy has contended that 90 percent of the press favored the Republican in part because of his considerations: "He treated the press as friends, as fellow journalists, in a way that sustained his dignity." These relationships proved to be possibly the most important for Harding's career. In 1880 the United States sported a population of 50,155,783, had 971 daily newspapers, and saw a daily circulation of 3,556,395 copies—one newspaper for every sixteen people. By 1920, with a population of 105,710,620 Americans, the country had 2,441 daily sheets and 33,028,630 papers in daily circulation—one newspaper for every three people despite the overall population more than doubling in the previous four decades.[27] The press did not just sustain the candidate's dignity, they propelled him to victory. It makes sense that if Harding really had 90 percent of the press behind him, then he could pull off 60 percent of the popular vote with the ubiquity of newspapers in the United States by 1920.

Frequently, the press and media projected images of the candidate that helped reinforce the idea that he was a hardworking "common man" even during the campaign. The *Memphis Commercial Appeal* wrote that Harding wanted to prove that he was "a real printer," so a motion picture camera captured images of him rolling up his sleeves as he "made up" the first page of the next morning's issue. The newspaper also took pictures of the workers who "gathered about to see their boss working while they loafed." Apparently, Harding "kept up a rapid fire of conversation with his foreman while working." There were also pictures taken of the candidate while he inspected the edition as it was initially coming off the printing press. Senator New also posed with him.[28] Front porch campaigning saw the candidate retain his dignity in the private sphere and continue "working hard" at the *Star*'s headquarters. People knew that Harding had stopped being a newspaper editor over two decades earlier, but the images helped convey the message that he could still understand working a job—like the dignified common man that his publicists wanted the voters to consume.

Not only was Harding a former newspaper editor, but he was also involved in multiple businesses in Marion. One campaign reporter noted that he had heard voters say recently that they wanted a businessman for president. He reminded his readers that Harding had served as a director of multiple institutions, including Marion's largest bank, a local building-and-loan company, a wholesale lumber company, a retail lumber and coal company, and a local telegraph company. The report claimed that Harding was also a stockholder as well as an affable guy willing to "forgo another hours sleep just to visit" another delegation.[29] Harding thus was a common man and an affable guy as well as an entrepreneur with business sense.

The press also molded the candidate's image around sports. Early in the campaign, he made the error of being shown playing golf, a game that was considered a wealthy man's sport and that voters associated with William Taft. For Harding, this was bad publicity. One senator saw a movie of Harding playing golf and claimed that he could not hear one clap in the entire theater. Always willing to toe the party line, the candidate agreed to play secretively. Other papers minimized the number of golf games that he was actually able to play during the campaign season and quoted him reminding folks that on Sunday he simply liked to go to church. To retain Harding's positive image through sports, Republicans started working out the details to bring baseball teams to Marion. The Chicago Cubs were easy to enlist because Lasker owned a share of the team. Finding an opponent proved to be more difficult, however, as several teams declined the invitation. The New York Giants' manager, John J. McGraw, turned down an invitation after he "kicked it over at the last minute because of his political alignment." After being rejected by the Giants, the Cincinnati Reds, and the Cleveland Indians, Lasker settled for a minor-league team, the Kerrigan Tailors. Several prominent sports figures attended the game, including Cubs president Bill Veeck and pitching legend Grover Cleveland Alexander. The candidate warmed up with Alexander on the field before the game. The *New York Tribune* noted that Harding caught several balls barehanded before a player gave him a glove; "He threw with such vigor that his hat bobbed around on top of his head and paid little heed to the wild yells of the crowd." Harding not only threw out the first pitch but also threw three pitches just to assure the national audience of his love for the game. When he walked off the field, he received a cheer that "only

Babe Ruth ordinarily gets on a ballfield." Following the contest, the candidate gave the team a speech in which he compared running the country to being on a sports team: "I like to think of America first. I want our country to float the championship pennant in the contest of human achievement. You can't win a ball game with a one man team. Maybe it's old fashioned, but I am for team play. I am opposing the one man play for the nation." He also criticized America's unpreparedness for war under Wilson, telling the players: "Nobody has confidence in a ball team that is untrained. National unpreparedness for war cost us many precious lives and endless billions in waste, and unpreparedness for peace is costing billions more and holding us in anxiety and uncertainty."[30]

Newsmen also captured the day that a delegation of entertainment stars came to town. Babe Ruth was rumored to be part of the entourage, but he did not visit.[31] The celebrities, calling themselves members of the Harding-Coolidge Theatrical League, were led by Al Jolson and included DeWolfe Hopper, Mary Pickford, Pearl White, Irene Castle, Henry Dixie, Leo Carillo, and Pauline Frederick. John Hand's 110-piece band from Chicago played "Hail, Hail, the Gang's All Here" as they escorted the visitors from the train depot to Harding's porch. The group waved banners that read, "Harding and Coolidge Theatrical League, 40,000 strong." Jolson, a mammy singer, sang for the presidential hopeful:

We think the country's ready for a man like Teddy,
One who is a fighter through and through,
We need another Lincoln to do the nation's thinking,
And Mr. Harding, we've selected you.

The rest of the singers joined in chorus:

Harding, lead the G.O.P.,
Harding, on to victory!
We're here to make a fuss,
Mr. Harding, you're the man for us.[32]

He also sent Harding an autographed copy of the song.

Cox, the Democratic candidate, tried to combat the positive publicity that Harding's visit with the entertainers generated. He visited a Hollywood studio on September 21 called First National Studios, where he tried to act in a movie titled *Aboard the Ship of State.* Cox apparently "disported a number of girls in bathing suits." The film was shown in all First National theaters but attracted no Hollywood stars in the viewing audience. Films of Harding, by contrast, attracted stars such as Ethel Barrymore and Jolson.[33]

Right before Harding's public appearance with the celebrities, one newspaper made sure to dress up a story about him and his acting career that illuminated his hardworking attitude and common-man persona. The paper explained that as a youth Harding was part of the Marion home-talent theatrical organization. One afternoon he finished work and took a train twenty-five miles to Marysville to play a role he had in *Don Cesar De Bazan.* Upon Harding's arrival, the theater manager told him that there would be no play that night because he had experienced some trouble with some of the visiting Marionites earlier that day. Since there was no return train scheduled that evening, Harding walked the twenty-five miles back to Marion so that he could attend work the next day.[34] The press labored to merchandize the Republican candidate as a man capable of schmoozing with talented athletes, actors, and entertainers while still highlighting his hardworking, blue-collar nature.

Not only did Harding meet with professional athletes and Hollywood entertainers, but the press also made sure to convey images of him befriending just about every visitor conceivable. Republican organizers orchestrated several events to provide ample demonstrations. In one instance the *Memphis Commercial Appeal* reported that the candidate met with "six barefoot Marion urchins" and their "cocky little leader" carrying an American flag along with a picture of Harding attached to the head of a snow shovel. The children sang a campaign song to the candidate, who responded by shaking their hands and smiling for a picture with each of them. A few weeks later Harding met with a navy recruiting band and reminded them that he used to play a horn growing up. He explained to the musicians that he had recently received a gift cornet from some Indiana instrument makers. A band member yelled out, "Well, sir, let's hear you play it." Harding replied: "It's been thirty years since I played. But I tell you what I'll do. I'll let you play it." He then signed the head of a snare drum and, when asked to sign the bass drum, remarked, "Well, here's a humdinger." His wife brought out the gift cornet, on which a member of the band played "Dardanella." On another occasion a campaign manager named Robert Armstrong bragged that in Marion both Democrats and Republicans "passed [money] into the hat" for their hometown candidate's campaign fund.[35] Stories about Harding meeting with band members or little children and receiving campaign donations from Democratic neighbors, along with images of him cozying up to professional baseball players and entertainers, created a nice mix of merchandizing material for the campaign.

Republican strategists knew that marketing was critical to success, but it was all for nothing without Harding's folksy personality and ability to make people feel comfortable with him. One Republican National Committee member from Maine, Guy Gannett, traveled to meet Harding, declaring afterward: "I've come back from Marion filled with the keenest enthusiasm over the personality of the Republican candidate for President. I do not know how to express it better than to say that Senator Harding impressed me as the kind of a man you would select to serve as executor of your estate." Gannett explained that politicians usually struck him as disingenuous, but "Harding impressed me exactly the other way; he struck me as a man of absolute sincerity. He is the kind of man I would gladly entrust with any responsibility in the world." The Maine Republican also liked the masculinity that the candidate's reserved, confident manner projected: "Senator Harding is very much of a man, and a man's man at that—and we have had enough of the near-man type of statesmanship lately to know how to appreciate Mr. Harding. He is not one of the loud shouting, promising anything type of politician, but quiet, reserved, thoughtful—a real statesmen." Gannett was equally impressed by the Ohioan's background, home, and reputation in Marion: "It has been clear all along that much of Senator Harding's fitness for office comes from the fact that he is of the people, from the people and for the people. As everybody knows, he was born a farm boy, has worked as a day laborer and has made his way through life, without aid or backing. He has never lost touch of the common people or their needs." He tied Harding's basic upbringing with his current house: "His very simplicity of thought and life is well known by his home at Marion. You never saw a more unpretentious residence—a plain story-and-a-half frame house. I could tell it was the home of the candidate for the presidency, not by its pretentiousness, but solely by the crowds around it. It is just such a home as you can see by the thousands in Maine—a narrow, simple, clapboard house with a piazza—the kind you could buy before the war. It takes a simple man, a man of the people, to live like that." Gannett also noted that Republicans and Democrats in Marion all liked Harding and that the people who worked for him were also "a happy family." Maine's state elections were held in mid-September 1920 and were overwhelmingly won by Republicans after voters had almost a year to think about Wilson's League of Nations proposal.[36]

Besides impressing political operatives, Harding's handlers also staged events that specifically invited women, African Americans, naturalized citizens, and first-time voters to meet the candidate. A delegation of Methodists, Baptists, and members of the Equal Rights League participated on what was advertised as "Colored Voters' Day." The Marion Negro Baptist Church provided a tent to shelter the group.[37] John Pershing, infamous for having his segregated black units fight before his white units during the Great War, happened to be at the Harding home that day. The general stated, "The colored people of America are to be congratulated upon their magnificent showing at home and abroad during the war, and we are all to be congratulated, for without that support we would not have been able to win the victory as early as we did." Newspapers joked that Pershing changed his religion twice that day: in the morning he became a Baptist and in the afternoon, a Methodist. Like Marion, Pershing welcomed African Americans on "Colored Voters' Day."

When McKinley had addressed African Americans in Canton, they had been experiencing life under Jim Crow segregation laws for seven years; by the time they came to visit Harding, they had endured this legalized repression for over a quarter of a century. From his porch Harding claimed that US citizenship was largely based on service and asserted that African Americans were doing their part. He proclaimed: "The American Negro has the good sense to know the truth . . . , that he has met the test and did not and will not fail America. . . . Brutal and unlawful violence, whether it proceeds from those who break the law or from those who take the law into their own hands, can only be dealt with in one way, by true Americans whether they be of your blood or of mine." Rumors had flown that Harding was actually a mixed-race candidate—he was trying to ingratiate himself with his listeners and simultaneously let his readership know that he was not a black man. Harding condemned the "brutal and unlawful violence" committed by "those who take the law into their own hands."[38] Just like his front porch predecessors, the senator offered up platitudes and false promises to African Americans as trends against them in American society continued to proliferate.

While Harding was inviting toward his African American visitors, he took a different tone with a delegation of naturalized citizens. He may have felt pressure to keep his distance because Democratic leaders, including vice presidential nominee Franklin Roosevelt, were publicly stating that Harding was courting the "hyphenated vote," as naturalized Americans were pejoratively characterized. The Republican's America First philosophy and his ability to tie that to protecting American homes and families was made evident in his rhetoric to his visitors: "Let us pray that America . . . shall never feel the menace of hyphenated citizenship. . . . For Americans who love America I sound a warning. It is not beyond possibility that the day might come—and may God forbid it—when an organized hyphenated vote in American politics might have the balance of voting power to elect our government. . . . I insist that the American conscience recognize the duty of protecting our national health. I insist that it will protect American motherhood and American child-hood and the American home. There can be no defense for working conditions which rob the American child of its rights." The title of this speech was "MUST PROTECT AMERICAN HOME."[39] Although his words sounded harsh, they most likely comforted the larger consuming audience of native-born Americans who had just endured a war on foreign soil. Harding understood that while he was probably making his personal audience uncomfortable, the speech would reach a larger audience that he was appealing to with such rhetoric couched in family and home protection, much like the words of McKinley.

While Harding spoke publicly about his dislike for the "hyphenated citizen-ship," he privately snubbed a visit from German Americans. Fairly confident that the candidate would garner their vote, one Republican insider wrote: "The Germans are largely with us. In fact, the German support in Ohio promises to offset the labor defection. The big German papers like the Staats-Zeitung here, are almost daily attacking Wilsonism." In August leaders from the German-American National Club endorsed Harding because of his "unalter-able opposition to the League of Nations and to the perfidious foreign policy." One of its leaders, Dr. H. Gerhard, asked if his group could visit Harding in Marion. He was "politely advised" to stay at home, despite the fact that Marion resident J. E. Phillips was a member of the German-American National Club.[40] Campaign organizers were acutely aware of the kinds of events that they wanted projected across the United States and those they did not want the consuming audience to consider. While Republicans wanted naturalized Germans' votes, they did not want images of Harding befriending them seen throughout the country so soon after the end of the war.

Although comfortable with silently snubbing German voters, Harding's or-ganizers were eager to make female voters a centerpiece of events in Marion. This was a necessary strategy resulting from the passage of the Nineteenth Amendment the year before: women would be voting nationwide for the first time in a presidential contest. Harding had an important image to project to them—that of a trustworthy family man. When the candidate met with vot-ers, he almost always had his wife, Florence, by his side. While she had been divorced once, she was Harding's first and only spouse. This helped his family man image with both men and women, especially when juxtaposed with Democrat James Cox, a man who had experienced a divorce just over a decade before the contest. In one talk Harding's sister reminded her audience that her brother had never been divorced. In further pursuit of a wholesome image, she noted that even though he owned stock in a brewery, he had received it to satisfy an unconnected debt and simply had never cashed it out.[41]

The press made sure that their readers were aware of the ubiquity of Harding's wife on the campaign trail, knowing that her active participation in the events could only help their man's bid for women's votes. One sheet highlighted that Florence was constantly by the candidate's side throughout his appearances, much like McKinley's spouse had been. She had received the nickname "Snowbird" from some Native American friends, which meant that she was a very hard worker, accessible to all, and truly genuine in her interactions with every visitor. The paper claimed that she graciously did most of the gift accepting for the couple, including blueberries from Indian River, sugar-cured ham from Virginia, peaches, watermelons, and cakes with the name "Harding" traced on top of them; frequently she replied to the gifts with a letter of thanks.[42] For Republican organizers, a key to staging and merchandizing campaign events effectively was positioning Harding's wife in a way that made her look active and made the family appear trustworthy.

Republicans editors were eager to compare Harding's marriage to Cox's divorce and remind voters that the difference would cost the Democrat votes. In early August the *Los Angeles Times* printed an interview done with judge Willis Vickery of Ohio, in which he described some details behind the case. Vickery claimed that Mrs. Cox had filed for divorce in July 1908 because of her husband's "gross neglection of duty," which he did not contest. The children went to live with their mother in Cleveland. Judge Vickery opined that the divorce would cost Cox "a million votes" with women who did not believe in divorce; the headline for the article read "THINKS WOMEN WILL BAR COX."[43] For some Republicans, branding Cox as a divorced man who had neglected his duties as a family man and husband was also critical to their merchandizing strategy.

The *Los Angeles Times* also liked to make Cox look desperate for women's votes as he traveled around the country. In one cartoon the paper showed a calm, pretty woman from Los Angeles shaking hands with a sweating Cox, clearly on the campaign trail meeting voters. The cartoon highlighted that while the Democrat shook her right hand, he had his hat turned upside down in his left hand as if begging for her vote. The caption over the picture jabbed, "Traveling for Your Health, Gov.?"[44] The *Times* and other outlets ran numerous pictures of Harding working at the printing press or posing with his wife and children. Projecting images of a trustworthy, hardworking family man versus cartoons lampooning a traveling, once-divorced man were perfect for the Republican image-making machine.

While Harding's handlers worked hard to craft his image with women across the country, women in Marion helped facilitate a front porch campaign for their favorite son. The Women's Harding for President Club started holding meetings in town about a week after his nomination to help plan out the campaign. They created an emergency-service committee to arrange for emergency canteen operations, which would be located conveniently and offer coffee and sandwiches, if the crowds became too large for the town's restaurants and hotels. The *Marion Star* claimed, "The plan is to have this canteen service worked out similar to that carried out during the war."[45] A few days later one hundred members of the female club canvassed the town looking for extra rooms for incoming overnight visitors. They provided cards to homeowners so they could record the accommodations they could provide. Early reports indicated that locals were willing to offer some of their "best rooms" for visitors to use. The director of the Ohio Republican Club, Walter Rodgers, asked that the club be invited to the state party meeting in Columbus later that summer.

Eleanor Margaret Freeland, a local schoolteacher, provided the Republican campaign with some highly consumable human-interest stories about the Harding home, the candidate, and his wife in a series of articles titled Girl Next Door to Hardings. In the first article Freeland described the coziness and level of hospitality in the Harding home: "Of course we all know that a lot of Mr. Harding's success is due to the way Mrs. Harding made the wheels go round in that little back kitchen of hers. I see where a lot of newspaper men wrote up about the fine waffles that she cooked for them, but it takes something more than waffles to run a house and keep a man hale and hearty, with only one little maid to help most of the time." She noted that the family welcomed additional house staff during the campaign but paid particular attention to the Hardings' longstanding chauffer and his wife and their relationship with the neighbors:

The other day her new help came; two cooks and a butler, besides Frank and Bernice. No one in Marion ever had a real butler before. He looks like the kind

you see in the movies—all dressed up for the part, and they tell me her cook
has been the envy of all Washington. Frank and Bernice are almost considered part of the family by the neighbors. Everyone on our street likes them,
they are so kind and friendly. Frank is Mr. Harding's chauffer and Bernice
is his pretty little French-looking wife. Of course, Frank is something more
than a mere chauffer, for he lived at the Hardings long before their move to
Washington and Mr. Harding once said he wouldn't run for President if he
couldn't have Frank to run his machine while he was running.[46]

Freeland portrayed the Harding family and the town of Marion as so tight-
knit that Frank and Bernice, a chauffeur and a cook, were not only part of
the family but also part of the larger community.

In her second article Freeland highlighted the folksiness of Mrs. Harding:
"Mrs. Harding herself came clear out to the auto to say good-bye to a very
distinguished looking gentleman, who we felt sure must be of great importance. Then she saw us and, will you believe it, she came right over and sat
on our porch and visited with us, just as nice and friendly. She wore a little
blue foulard silk dress, and looked neat and dignified. I noticed that she wasn't
wearing any flashy rings, and if she did have powder on I couldn't see it."
Freeland also described the level of poise that Mrs. Harding displayed while
running the home during the busy campaign: "When the movie men come
or the press photographers, she doesn't fuss up, but just leaves the backyard
where she is cutting roses, or the back-porch where she is showing the butler
how to polish the silver, and goes right out and poses and smiles and talks
and doesn't seem a bit excited. It surely hasn't gone to her head about being
the First Lady of the Land."[47]

While positive press coverage from friendly neighbors helped merchandize the Harding brand, the candidate himself conducted several tricky
meetings with delegations concerned about women's suffrage—Harding
frequently straddled the political fence on the issue. Despite the passage
of the Nineteenth Amendment, the Tennessee legislature was still debating
its ratification in their state. Just before notification day, newspapers made
public Harding's willingness to meet with an antisuffrage delegation called
the National Association Opposed to Woman Suffrage. The candidate wrote to
the group that he would "readily" meet "those who are opposed to women's
suffrage" and that he "did not mean to be a candidate who is the partisan
toward any particular group in our American activities." The letter was made
public by the organization on July 15. Less than a week later, Alice Paul led a

group of one hundred "militant" women, many of them prominent suffrage leaders from around the country, to Harding's front porch. They wore white outfits with purple, gold, and white regalia and carried the Woman's Party tricolored banner. Delegations from different states in the group carried different banners along with purple, gold, and white banners.[48] There is no evidence that the women interacted with the senator. Yet it is almost certain that the "militant" women knew of Harding's offer to meet the antisuffrage group just a week earlier. But a meeting between Harding and angry women one year after the passage of the Nineteenth Amendment was a campaign nightmare to be carefully avoided by his handlers.

When Harding did receive female delegations, he framed his position on women's suffrage in reference to his own party and its importance in the ratification process. After receiving a visit from the American Women's Suffrage Association, he sent a telegram to its president, Carrie Chapman Mott, stating, "I am exceedingly glad to learn you are in Tennessee seeking to consummate the ratification of the equal suffrage amendment. If any of the Republican members of the Tennessee assembly should ask my opinion to their course, I would cordially recommend an immediate favorable action." Later reports stated that Harding was having "more suffrage troubles." When he received a visit from Mott asking him "to do something more" about the situation in Tennessee, he replied: "No discouragement is voiced from here. On the contrary we are continuing to encourage the Republicans of the Tennessee general assembly to join cordially in efforts to consummate ratification." Following the visit, the candidate wired the chairman of the Republican state committee in Tennessee, "I cling to the belief . . . that in Tennessee Republicans are in a position to serve both party and country by effecting ratification."[49]

While interjecting the party's name into all discussions concerning women's suffrage, Harding also pled with female voters not to vote against male candidates who had previously voted against women's suffrage. Speaking to a group of voters in late August, he "asked them not to 'measure a man by rule' of whether he supported suffrage, but to judge him by his whole record." Harding stated that "it was silly to expect women to vote according to the politics of the state that perfected ratification, and reminded them that if it had not been for the twenty-nine Republican states that first voted for suffrage there would have been no need for Tennessee." Earlier he had reminded women to "not make the mistake of separating into sex groups. Woman must come into the political parties and make them what they ought to be. I think I know which party they will come into. Don't imagine politics is a muddy pool. It is the finest most patriotic business in the United States. You must make your party represent your ideals. Come on in; the water's fine."⁵⁰ Like those before him, Harding habitually offered up platitudes to women and African Americans without making any concrete promises about a better future to either group.

Harding also liked to single out women when he articulated his position against US participation in the League of Nations. Speaking to a large group of women, he stated that "the mothers and wives of America do not wish to give their sons and husbands for sacrifice at the call of an extra-constitutional body like the council of the league." On another occasion the candidate explained that when it came to foreign affairs, "I thank God that the time has come when I can ask the advice of American women and especially the mothers of America." Finally, on the last day of his front porch campaign, Harding explained how important he thought women were in helping the United States understand its proper place in the international community: "First to the women I declare my faith. Greta indeed must be the contribution which you and all of the women of America will make not only to move us to a wiser sympathy and tenderness in our own special fabric at home and our humane relationships with other nations and other peoples, but also to restrain from the folly of wasteful impulse. . . . America expects you to keep this Republic and the American home kind and keep America sensitive to their obligations to the world." The final day of homebound campaigning in Marion was supposed to feature first-time voters, but it became "largely a women's demonstration." The "remarkable" number of women combined with first-time male voters from twenty institutions made Marion lively with songs and yells. The *Los Angeles Times* claimed that this final campaign day was characterized by youthful exuberance.⁵¹

While Harding tied his anti–League of Nations stance to his support for American families, Cox's detractors managed to tie his divorce to his support for that international body. In early September one sheet printed a cartoon of the single Cox walking down the aisle with his new bride-to-be, a woman with a dress titled "League of Nations" and holding a marriage certificate in her hand. The paper commented that she had a short veil "suitable for a widow." The "bride" also had fourteen children, mocking the Fourteen Points Wilson wanted after the war. The child identified as number ten had on a devil's mask with a smirk, deriding the treaty stipulation that guaranteed Austria-Hungary freedom and autonomy despite its heavy influence in starting the war. Holding a bewildered-looking Cox by the wrist, the "bride" is shown stating to the children, "Now, children this is your new papa." Looking at the

Democratic candidate, the children collectively say, "Lo Pop." Cox is shown stating, "Can't we have separate homes like Fannie Hurst," in reference to the popular writer and women's rights advocate. Three small men labeled "The Ushers" depicting prominent Democrats Bernard Baruch, the financial advisor for Woodrow Wilson and later famous New Dealer; William Jamieson, a newspaper publisher and Democratic representative in the House; and W. L. Chadbourne, who helped Cox secure the Democratic nomination in Dayton, stand right behind the "groom" asking for campaign donations. Two long-fingered hands reach out in the top of the background with the caption, "May I not now pronounce you man and wife?" Over the top of the cartoon is a description of the scene: "THE FATAL WEDDING, or, aint nobody going to kiss the bride? The hero, an Ohio product, in a moment of abstraction, is grabbed by a widder with fourteen kids and before help can arrive is united to the entire outfit, they are now on their wedding trip. His [Cox's] voice says 'I'm happy' but his face says 'darn it!'"[52]

The dual strategy of creating positive events in Marion and then broadcasting and marketing them to a consuming audience seemed to be highly effective for Republicans. Harding's front porch campaign was the fourth to win as well as the most successful ever, garnering 60.3 percent of the popular vote. But his journey was different than his predecessors. While the first three Republicans winning with this technique had mostly stayed on their front porches, Harding toured multiple states. Historian Randolph Downes focused on the waning effectiveness of the front porch campaign as the summer of 1920 wore on, stressing that it ended on October 18, right after which Harding hit the road like Cox. For Downes, the front porch performances became "boring, and their publicity value declined." While Republican leaders changed the everyday nature of Harding's schedule to a series of "Super Days," at the end "what really happened was the abandonment of the front-porch campaign."[53]

As Downes has argued, Harding's managers probably took the importance of his porch campaign too seriously. Lasker's chief counsel, Richard Child, penned a telling letter to Hays in September explaining the importance of crowds to homebound campaigning: "As I see it, we are winners unless there be breaks or sags. But mark it Will—I see a real danger in the possibility of an anti-climax to the porch campaign." He also speculated about the next six weeks of the campaign: "We have about forty-five days to go, and it would be serious, if the porch campaign part of the period did not assume increasing bigness and pungency." Commenting on the importance of big crowds, he wrote that the "mere frequency of visiting delegations is even undesirable unless they represent big things and give us a chance to say big things." He disappointedly admitted that "it has been enough for this organization here to sit behind a cigar and wait for delegations [to] apply. Except for a few occasions, which have been definitely 'worked up,' I do not think much of the results." Child worried about the size and vitality of future delegations to Marion: "Inconsequential occasions give no inspiration to a candidate. . . . [T]he delegation business must not drift. It must be stage managed by men of capacity. Hereafter let's avoid the petty delegations and picayune occasions, and get big publicity material." Finally, he boldly predicted, "If we don't [do that] the middle of October will see the campaign without any fault of the candidate, sag like an old empty hammock."[54] Republican campaigners were clearly aware that if not enough people attended their events, then lack of attendance would become the actual event and the story portrayed for consumption. By mid-October, Harding was out stumping and competing with Cox on the road. The front porch had been left behind.

The Stump Eclipses the Porch

Following Harding's effort, no presidential candidate has conducted a front porch campaign. The 1920s saw a series of men, including John Davis, Al Smith, and Herbert Hoover, go on tours considerably less inspiring than those of Theodore Roosevelt and William Jennings Bryan. In the 1930s the nation was experiencing its worst-ever depression, so holding a front porch campaign would have been impractical and out of touch with voters' realities. In the 1940s the United States mobilized for another war overseas—a front porch campaign then would have come off as wasteful and unpatriotic. Voter interest also plummeted: while Gilded Age presidential campaigns saw between 70 and 80 percent turnout on Election Day, by 1920 that rate had dropped to 49 percent. Being heckled on the road seemed less embarrassing in the 1920s than holding a homebound campaign hosting tiny delegations. In addition to historical circumstances, improvements in transportation, the rise of radio, improvements in mass-marketing skills, and the continued proliferation of newspapers all made people used to things coming to them, not the other way around. Speeches and candidates could be reproduced in voters' living rooms, so why travel to meet the person? This technological process culminated in the 1950s with the rise of television—and it continues today with the internet.

Front porch campaigning holds a unique place in American political history. There has never been a presidential-campaign technique that has been so successful and then disappeared so quickly and thoroughly. It originated at a time when the state of presidential campaigning was in flux. Men were trying to figure out how to seem appropriately interested in office while avoiding being disproportionally aggressive—the front porch and their homes allowed Garfield, Harrison, McKinley, and Harding to do just that. Homebound campaigning allowed these men to balance the antiquated notions of honor and dignity that the Founding Fathers possessed while reaching out to the electorate by talking to voters, shaking their hands, mingling with them publicly, and having these actions splashed across newspapers around the country. The promise of high protective tariffs allowed for their message to fit perfectly with the homebound style. Not only did the porch campaigns transform the candidates, but it also changed the midwestern "island communities" in which they ran, especially Indianapolis and Canton. While these changes appeared exciting to outside observers, the folks that lived in the small cities faced a series of challenges themselves.

In 1880 Garfield had no idea that he was setting an effective trend for future Republicans when he started interacting with groups of visitors from his porch in Mentor, Ohio. After winning a close contest, he entered office with a lot of hope. Unfortunately, Garfield was assassinated four months after his inauguration. A town with a population of 540 in 1880, Mentor is now a city with over 47,000 people. In 2010 CNNMoney.com ranked it thirty-seventh among the one hundred "Best Places to Live in America."

Eight years later Harrison used his front porch to help make himself more likable. In the process the residents of Indianapolis saw hundreds of thousands of visitors march down their streets. While the rural town of Mentor held a bucolic, tame front porch campaign, the Indiana capital hosted large crowds and delegations that displayed a great deal of pageantry. Harrison eventually lost a rematch election to Cleveland in 1892 and left the White House to return to his Indiana front porch. But the city of 75,000 folks in 1888 would grow, according to the 2010 Census, to have over 820,000 residents. Indianapolis is now the thirteenth-largest city in the United States.

The campaign in Mentor seemed like a picnic compared to what Canton experienced in 1896. Through it all, McKinley defeated one of the greatest stump speakers in American history from his porch. He went on to become one of the most important US presidents; the second-worst depression in the country's history ended and the Spanish-American War took place under his administration. Ironically, McKinley used the front porch to become the president, but his assassination gave rise to Teddy Roosevelt, whose stumping ability helped end front porch campaigning. Growing modestly from its nearly 40,500 residents in 1896, Canton now has a population of 73,000 (according to the 2010 Census) but, thanks to the Pro Football Hall of Fame, remains a travel destination.

In 1920 Marion seemed more like Mentor than Indianapolis or Canton, with its bucolic setting and lack of crime. Harding's message of "Back to Normalcy" meshed well with running from the small town. Marion held glitzy parades and sported a gaudy candidate. Harding died two years into office and was replaced by Calvin Coolidge. A town of almost 28,000 in 1920, Marion has grown the least of the four places that hosted front porch campaigns, having 36,000 residents, according to the 2010 Census.

The bucolic, small-town settings provided by the four Republican candidates residences were perfect stages for local campaign events that newspapers could report across a rapidly industrializing country. The towns made a large, impersonal process seem personable and folksy at a time when economic development was making ideas and feelings associated with personability and folksiness disappear for many.

While front porch campaigns changed the towns that hosted them, the process also transformed the Republican Party. Since its entrance into national politics in the mid-1850s, the party had been engaged in the long-term process of centralizing itself behind strong candidates. Front porch campaigning played a critical role in moving that process forward as Republicans were able to come together behind one man in one town for a sustained period of time. Their ability to organize their political efforts around the candidate and the town and produce events for newspapers to describe across the country proved to be important for the growth of the party and provided a winning formula for partisan success on the national level.

Just as Republicans were centralizing behind strong, homebound candidate in the 1880s and 1890s, the economy was industrializing and branding products was becoming a popular technique to increase profits. By 1888 Republican managers realized that merchandising their candidate as a brand was helpful in generating votes on Election Day. Republicans continued to effectively brand in 1896, when McKinley won despite the fact that Democrat Bryan was extremely talented at speechmaking and gave charismatic talks across major portions of the country. In the 1880s and 1890s, newspapers and pamphlets did the merchandising; by 1920, Republicans were also employing the phonograph to market their man. The ability to use the media to effectively brand their candidates transformed the Republican Party and the way that campaigns have been run since—selling an active candidate remains a well-regarded strategy in national politics in the twenty-first century.

Notes

INTRODUCTION

1. *Indianapolis Journal,* July 23, 1888.

2. William Henry Harrison stumped for the presidency in 1840 and won.

3. Harry B. Carrington, "Winfield Scott's Visit to Columbus," *Ohio Archeological and Historical Quarterly* 19 (July 1910): 285; *New York Times,* Sept. 13, 1860.

4. Robert Wiebe, *The Search for Order, 1877–1920* (New York: Hill & Wang, 1967), vii; Gil Troy, *See How They Ran: The Changing Role of the Presidential Candidate* (Cambridge, MA: Harvard Univ. Press, 1996), 96.

5. Charles Calhoun points out that Republicans added a plank to their 1880 platform eliminating polygamy, which was being practiced by Mormons in Utah. See Calhoun, *From Bloody Shirt to Full Dinner Pail: The Transformation of Politics and Governance in the Gilded Age* (New York: Hill & Wang, 2010), 70.

6. Rebecca Edwards, *Angels in the Machinery: Gender in American Party Politics from the Civil War to the Progressive Era* (New York: Oxford Univ. Press, 1997), 19–35, 75–90 (quotes, 26, 33).

7. Michael McGerr, *The Decline of Popular Politics: The American North, 1865–1928* (New York: Oxford Univ. Press, 1985), 69–106.

8. Nina Silber, *The Romance of Reunion: Northerners and the South, 1865–1900* (Chapel Hill: Univ. of North Carolina Press, 1993), 97; Benjamin Harrison, *Speeches of Benjamin Harrison . . . ,* comp. Charles Hedges (New York: United States Book, 1892), 84.

9. *New York Times,* Oct. 19, 1880; *New York Herald,* Oct. 19, 1880; *Chicago Tribune,* Oct. 19, 1880; H. Wayne Morgan, *From Hayes to McKinley: National Party Politics, 1877–1896* (Syracuse, NY: Syracuse Univ. Press, 1969), 307.

10. *Chicago Tribune,* Aug. 2, 1888; *New York Herald,* Oct. 6, 1888; *Cleveland Plain Dealer,* Sept. 28, 1896.

I. GERMANS, JUBILEE SINGERS, AND AXE MEN

An earlier version of this chapter was published under the same title in *Ohio History* 121 (2014): 112–29. It is used here with permission.

1. Joseph Stanley-Brown, "My Friend Garfield," *American Heritage* 22, no. 5 (Aug. 1971): 49–53, 100–101.

2. For a brief summary of the early front porch campaigns, see Troy, *See How They Ran*, 86–117. Troy treats Garfield's campaign with an extremely brief analysis on the bottom of page 89 and the top of page 90.

3. Morgan, *From Hayes to McKinley*, 105–6.

4. Troy, *See How They Ran*, 78; *New York Tribune*, Nov. 8, 1876.

5. Michael McGerr explains the rise of the spectacle political style in *Decline of Popular Politics*, 12–41.

6. For a concise summary of the Republican nominating convention in 1880, see Allan Peskin, *Garfield: A Biography* (Kent, OH: Kent State Univ. Press, 1978), 462–81. For a more recent treatment of the convention, see Kenneth Ackerman, *Dark Horse: The Surprise Election and Political Murder of President James A. Garfield* (New York: Carroll & Graf, 2004), 53–122.

7. For more on the life of Garfield, see Peskin, *Garfield*, or Ackerman, *Dark Horse*. For an older yet still useful look at Garfield, see Theodore Clarke-Smith, *The Life and Letters of James Abram Garfield*, 2 vols. (New Haven, CT: Yale Univ. Press, 1925).

8. William Balch, *The Life of James Abram Garfield, Late President of the United States*. . . . (Philadelphia: J. C. McCurdy, 1881), 320, 321; James D. McCabe, *Our Martyred President . . . : The Life and Public Services of General James A. Garfield*. . . . (Philadelphia: National Publishing, 1881), 515; A. F. Rockwell, "From Mentor to Elberon," *Century Magazine* 23, 433.

9. McCabe, *Our Martyred President*, 520; *New York Herald*, Oct. 9, 1880; James A. Garfield, *The Diary of James A. Garfield*, ed. H. J Brown and F. D. Williams, vol. 4 (East Lansing: Michigan State Univ. Press, 1981), 460–61.

10. C. E. Fuller, *Reminiscences of James A. Garfield* (Cincinnati: Standard, 1887), 430.

11. Clarke-Smith, *Life and Letters of James Abram Garfield*, 2:1038; Garfield, *Diary*, 452; *Painesville (OH) Telegraph*, Sept. 9, 1880; *Indianapolis Journal*, Sept. 5, 1880; *Springfield (MA) Republican*, Sept. 5, 1880; *New York Times*, Sept. 5, 1880; *Chicago Tribune*, Sept. 5, 1880.

12. Garfield, *Diary*, 452; *Indianapolis Journal*, Sept. 5, 6, 1880; *Painesville (OH) Telegraph*, Sept. 9, 1880; Leonard Dinnerstein, "Election of 1880," in *History of American Presidential Elections, 1848–1896*, ed. Arthur M. Schlesinger Jr., 4 vols. (New York: Chelsea House, 1971), 2:1509.

13. For the most recent analysis of Harrison's public stances on issues, see Charles Calhoun, *Minority Victory: Gilded Age Politics and the Front-Porch Campaign* (Lawrence: Univ. Press of Kansas, 2008), 132–34. For a treatment of McKinley's public pronouncements on issues, see R. Hal Williams, *Realigning America: McKinley, Bryan, and the Remarkable Election of 1896* (Lawrence: Univ. Press of Kansas, 2010), 140–41.

14. Troy, *See How They Ran*, 87, 88; *Indianapolis Journal*, Sept. 23, 1880; *Albany*

Evening Journal, Aug. 9, Sept. 29, Oct. 1, 1880; *Paterson (NJ) Daily Guardian,* Oct. 11, 1880; *New York Times,* Oct. 19, 1880; Thomas Clancy, *The Presidential Election of 1880* (Chicago: Loyola Univ. Press, 1958), 221.

15. Garfield, *Diary,* 459–62; *New York Times,* Sept. 29, 1880.

16. *Painesville (OH) Telegraph,* Sept. 30, 1880. For more full coverage of this interlude, see *New York Times,* Sept. 29, 1880.

17. Garfield, *Diary,* 462. Democratic organs started a rumor that Conkling and Garfield had a secret meeting on September 28 and reached what became known as the "Treaty of Mentor," in which Garfield promised Conkling patronage favors in return for his support during the election. Garfield does not mention this in his diary, and historians agree that no such arrangement was ever reached by the two men. See Peskin, *Garfield,* 501.

18. Clarke-Smith, *Life and Letters of James Abram Garfield,* 2:1033.

19. Clarke-Smith, *Life and Letters of James Abram Garfield,* 2:1038; *New York Herald,* Oct. 9, 1880; *New York Times,* Oct. 9, 1880; *Indianapolis Journal,* Oct. 9, 1880; *Chicago Tribune,* Oct. 9, 1880; *Springfield (MA) Republican,* Oct. 9, 1880.

20. Richard J. Jensen, *The Winning of the Midwest: Social and Political Conflict, 1888–1896* (Chicago: Univ. of Chicago Press, 1971), 6.

21. *Painesville (OH) Telegraph,* Oct. 14, 1880.

22. Calhoun, *From Bloody Shirt to Full Dinner Pail,* 73–74.

23. Charles Calhoun points out that during the Maine state election in mid-September, Republicans had done well in manufacturing towns but not shipping towns, which showed them how much traction the tariff issue had. The party thereafter started to stress protectionism. See *From Bloody Shirt to Full Dinner Pail,* 73–74.

24. Edwards contends that Democrats employed race-based reasons to rationalize themselves as protectors of the home by claiming to have to shield white laborers' wives from violent, malcontented black men. Edwards, *Angels in the Machinery,* 3–11.

25. This process is described in Edwards, *Angels in the Machinery,* 3–11. Beginning in 1881, the Prohibition Party claimed that protection of the home and family was at the root of their anti-alcohol positons.

26. Dinnerstein, "Election of 1880," 1509; Clarke-Smith, *Life and Letters of James Abram Garfield,* 2:1036–37.

27. Troy, *See How They Ran,* 84; Clarke-Smith, *Life and Letters of James Abram Garfield,* 2:1038; *New York Herald,* Oct. 16, 1880; *New York Times,* Oct. 16, 1880; *Chicago Tribune,* Oct. 16, 1880; *Indianapolis Journal,* Oct. 16, 1880.

28. Mark W. Summers, *Party Games: Getting, Keeping, and Using Power in Gilded Age Politics* (Chapel Hill: Univ. of North Carolina Press, 2004), 31; *Charleston (SC) News and Courier,* Nov. 2, 1880; Calhoun, *From Bloody Shirt to Full Dinner Pail,* 67, 73; David Blight, *Race and Reunion: The Civil War in American Memory* (Cambridge, MA: Belknap Press of Harvard Univ. Press, 2001), 52. Such comments in support of African American rights were also important as Garfield's opponent, Winfield Hancock, was seen as having been soft on Reconstruction. While commanding and governing Louisiana and Texas in 1867, Hancock had issued General Order 40, which placed the authority over criminal cases in those districts into civil, rather than military, courts.

In addition, Garfield was probably aware that the Greenback Party had actually adopted African American suffrage as a plank of their platform at their convention on June 9–11, 1880.

29. *Painesville (OH) Telegraph,* Oct. 21, 1880; Dinnerstein, "Election of 1880," 1508.

30. *Cleveland Herald,* Oct. 16, 1880; *Painesville (OH) Telegraph,* Oct. 21, 28, 1880.

31. *Cleveland Plain Dealer,* Oct. 16, 18, 20, 1880.

32. *Cleveland Plain Dealer,* Oct. 20, 1880. It is important when reading Gilded Age newspapers to remember that each one was partisan and made no attempt to appear unbiased before the public. By 1880 newspapers were either staunchly Democratic or Republican. The *New York Herald* had been supporting Republican candidates since the inception of the party, so it praised Garfield's front porch campaign from the beginning. The *Plain Dealer* was firmly a Democratic organ by 1880, so it criticized virtually every move that Garfield made. Of course, the papers took the opposite stance on the positions and movements of Hancock.

33. Clarke-Smith, *Life and Letters of James Abram Garfield,* 2:1037–38; *Indianapolis Journal,* Oct. 19, 1880; *New York Herald,* Oct. 19, 1880; *New York Times,* Oct. 19, 1880; *Chicago Tribune,* Oct. 19, 1880; *Painesville (OH) Telegraph,* Oct. 21, 1880.

34. *Cleveland Herald,* Oct. 19, 21, 1880.

35. *Indianapolis Journal,* Oct. 20, 1880; *New York Herald,* Oct. 20, 1880.

36. Dinnerstein, "Election of 1880," 1509; *Chicago Tribune,* Oct. 20, 1880; *New York Herald,* Oct. 20, 1880.

37. *Springfield (MA) Republican,* Oct. 20, 1880; *Washington Post,* Oct. 20, 1880; *New York Herald,* Oct. 20, 1880.

38. *New York Herald,* Oct. 20, 1880; *Indianapolis Journal,* Oct. 20, 1880.

39. *Indianapolis Journal,* Oct. 21, 1880; *New York Herald,* Oct. 21, 1880; *Springfield (MA) Republican,* Oct. 21, 1880; *New York Times,* Oct. 21, 1880; *Washington Post,* Oct. 21, 1880; *Chicago Tribune,* Oct. 21, 1880.

40. *Washington Post,* Oct. 21, 1880; *Cleveland Plain Dealer,* Oct. 22, 1880; *Cleveland Herald,* Oct. 21, 1880.

41. *Springfield (MA) Republican,* Oct. 21, 1880.

42. *Indianapolis Journal,* Oct. 22, 1880; *New York Herald,* Oct. 22, 1880; *Cleveland Herald,* Oct. 22, 26, 1880; *Springfield (MA) Republican,* Oct. 22, 1880; *New York Times,* Oct. 22, 1880; *Chicago Tribune,* Oct. 22, 1880.

43. Blight, *Race and Reunion,* 2.

44. Edwards, *Angels in the Machinery,* 29.

45. *Indianapolis Journal,* Oct. 27, 1880; *Springfield (MA) Republican,* Oct. 27, 1880; *New York Times,* Oct. 27, 1880; *New York Herald,* Oct. 27, 1880; *Chicago Tribune,* Oct. 27, 1880; *Cleveland Herald,* Oct. 27, 1880.

46. *Indianapolis Journal,* Oct. 28, 1880; *Cleveland Herald,* Oct. 28, 1880; *New York Herald,* Oct. 28, 1880; *New York Times,* Oct. 28, 1880; *Chicago Tribune,* Oct. 28, 1880.

47. Clarke-Smith, *Life and Letters of James Abram Garfield,* 2:1021–22. In Garfield's response to Anthony about women's suffrage, he argued that he did not think the majority of women actually wanted the right to vote. He also noted that since the Republican Party had not brought up the idea of women's suffrage as a plank in their

official platform, he really had no business bringing up the issue—he was merely the representative of the party and its stated interests. Garfield made none of this known during his speech to the women at Lawnfield.

48. *Cleveland Herald,* Oct. 28, 1880.

49. Edwards, *Angels in the Machinery,* 53.

50. Edwards, *Angels in the Machinery,* 26; Frederick E. Goodrich, *Life and Public Services of Winfield Scott Hancock, Military-General, U.S.A.* (Boston: Lee & Shepard, 1880), 330. Ironically, four years later the Democratic Party would lead the effort toward educational campaigns.

51. *New York Times,* Oct. 31, 1880. The number 329 was significant for Garfield during the election of 1880 for several reasons. The 3 represented Garfield's three years in the army, the 2 signified his two years in the Ohio Senate, and the 9 reflected his number of terms in Congress. The use of 329 by the Republican Party was also a direct rebuke of the Democrats use of the number, which represented Garfield's alleged take ($329) in the Credit Mobilier scandal. For further explanation, see Ackerman, *Dark Horse,* 219.

52. *New York Herald,* Oct. 31, 1880; *New York Times,* Oct. 31, 1880; *Washington Post,* Oct. 31, 1880; *Chicago Tribune,* Oct. 31, 1880; *Cleveland Herald,* Nov. 1, 1880.

53. *Cleveland Herald,* Nov. 1, 1880; *New York Herald,* Oct. 31, 1880.

54. Clarke-Smith, *Life and Letters of James Abram Garfield,* 2:1038–39. Mark Summers explains the popularity of military analogies in Gilded Age politics in *Party Games,* 33–53. Richard Jensen also notes the trend in *Winning of the Midwest,* 11.

55. *New York Times,* Oct. 31, 1880; *Indianapolis Journal,* Oct. 31, 1880; *New York Herald,* Oct. 31, 1880.

56. *New York Herald,* Nov. 1, 1880; Garfield, *Diary,* 479; *Painesville (OH) Telegraph,* Nov. 11, 1880; Dinnerstein, "Election of 1880," 1558.

57. *Cleveland Plain Dealer,* Oct. 20, 1880.

58. *Cleveland Plain Dealer,* Oct. 26, 1880.

59. Royal Cortissoz, *The Life of Whitelaw Reid,* vol. 2 (London: Thornton Butterworth Limited), 29, 32.

60. James G. Blaine, *Eulogy on James A. Garfield* (New York: J. S. Ogilvie, 1881), 9.

61. Rockwell, "From Mentor to Elberon," 433.

2. TRAINS, CANES, AND HANDSHAKES

An earlier version of this chapter was published as "Trains, Canes, and Replica Log Cabins: Benjamin Harrison's 1888 Front-Porch Campaign for the Presidency," *Indiana Magazine of History* 110 (Sept. 2014): 246–69. Revised and used here with permission.

1. *Indianapolis Sun,* June 25, 1888; *Chicago Tribune,* June 26, 1888.

2. Harry Sievers, *Hoosier Statesman: From the Civil War to the White House, 1865–1888,* vol. 2 of *Benjamin Harrison* (New York: Univ. Publishers, 1959), 127; Calhoun, *Minority Victory,* 87, 132–34. Sievers provides the most in-depth analysis of Harrison's front porch campaign; see *Hoosier Statesman,* 374–90. For the best book on

the election of 1888, see Calhoun, *Minority Victory.* For the most recent biography on Harrison, see Charles W. Calhoun, *Benjamin Harrison* (New York: Times Books–Henry Holt, 2005).

3. McGerr, *Decline of Popular Politics,* 69–106.

4. Calhoun, *Minority Victory,* 87.

5. *Springfield (MA) Republican,* July 1, 1888; Calhoun, *Minority Victory,* 88.

6. Sievers, *Hoosier Statesmen,* 358; Calhoun, *Minority Victory,* 89.

7. Calhoun, *Minority Victory,* 119. For a thorough look at the convention, see *Minority Victory,* 102–20.

8. For a concise look at any of the elections from 1840 through 1888, see Arthur M. Schlesinger Jr., ed., *History of American Presidential Elections, 1848–1896,* 4 vols. (New York: Chelsea House, 1971): for the elections of 1788 through 1848, see volume 1; for the elections of 1852 through 1896, see volume 2. For the best book on the evolution of presidential campaigning in the nineteenth century, see Troy, *See How They Ran.* The most current work on McKinley's campaign in 1896 is Williams, *Realigning America;* for McKinley's efforts from his front porch, see 129–45. For the most recent book on the election of 1884, see Mark W. Summers, *Rum, Romanism, and Rebellion: The Making of a President, 1884* (Chapel Hill: Univ. of North Carolina Press, 2000). Older important works on Gilded Age politics and the era's political culture include Richard Hofstadter, *The American Political Tradition and the Men Who Made It* (New York: Alfred A. Knopf, 1948); Morgan, *From Hayes to McKinley;* Robert D. Marcus, *Grand Old Party: Political Structure in the Gilded Age, 1880–1896* (New York: Oxford Univ. Press, 1971); Schlesinger, *History of American Presidential Elections;* and R. Hal Williams, *Years of Decision: American Politics in the 1890s* (New York: John Wiley and Sons, 1978). More recent important books on Gilded Age politics include Joel Silbey, *The American Political Nation, 1838–1893* (Stanford, CA: Stanford Univ. Press, 1991); Robert W. Cherny, *American Politics in the Gilded Age, 1868–1900* (Wheeling, IL: Harlan Davidson, 1997); Alan Ware, *The Democratic Party Heads North, 1877–1962* (New York: Cambridge Univ. Press, 2006); and Calhoun, *From Bloody Shirt to Full Dinner Pail.*

9. Rev. P. A. Tracy to B. Harrison, July 9, 1888, Benjamin Harrison Papers, Library of Congress, vol. 33; Calhoun, *Minority Victory,* 132–33.

10. *Harper's Weekly,* Aug. 11, 1888, 604; *Washington Post,* July 5, 1888; *Indianapolis Sun,* June 29, 1888; *Saint Louis Dispatch,* July 1, 1888; *Indianapolis Sentinel,* June 27, 1888; *Indianapolis Journal,* July 5, 1888.

11. Harrison, *Speeches,* 57; *Indianapolis Journal,* July 26, 1888; *Saint Louis Dispatch,* Sept. 16, 1888.

12. *Harper's Weekly,* Aug. 11, 1888, 601; B. R. Sulgrove, *History of Indianapolis and Marion County, Indiana* (Philadelphia: L. H. Everts, 1884), 17.

13. *Harper's Weekly,* Aug. 11, 1888, 601; *Indianapolis Journal,* July 18, 1888; Sulgrove, *History of Indianapolis and Marion County,* 20; *Washington Post,* Nov. 2, 1888; *Springfield (MA) Republican,* Sept. 23, 1888.

14. John Sherman to Harrison, July 13, 1888, Harrison Papers, vol. 33; Calhoun, *Minority Victory,* 126–27; Morgan, *From Hayes to McKinley,* 306; Harrison to Quay, Sept. 6, 1888, Matthew Stanley Quay Papers, Library of Congress, Washington, DC.

15. Calhoun, *Minority Victory,* 128.

16. McGerr, *Decline of Popular Politics,* 79; Calhoun, *Minority Victory,* 83, 95, 104.

17. In February 1889 the group renamed itself and officially incorporated as the Columbia Club. Its third, and current, headquarters is a landmark on Monument Circle.

18. Sievers, *Hoosier Statesmen,* 372.

19. Sievers, *Hoosier Statesmen,* 362.

20. Calhoun, *From Bloody Shirt to Full Dinner Pail,* 105–6, 116; *Chicago Tribune,* Aug. 19, 1888. The gifts that Harrison received were extremely varied, from butter to hair oil to a live eagle. Some of them referenced his position on the tariff, such as umbrellas to protect the economy or canes to prop it up. Other gifts were full of historical symbolism: for instance, Harrison received a replica log cabin, which symbolized his grandfather's run as a Whig in 1840 as the Log Cabin/Hard Cider candidate. He also received a battle flag from the 21st Illinois Infantry—Grant's original regiment at the beginning of the Civil War.

21. *Indianapolis Journal,* July 6, 1888.

22. *Chicago Tribune,* Sept. 16, 1888.

23. Harrison, *Speeches,* 125.

24. Summers, *Party Games,* 35.

25. *Chicago Tribune,* Aug. 18, 1888; Summers, *Party Games,* 41.

26. *Indianapolis Sun,* July 4, 1888; *Springfield (MA) Republican,* July 1, 1888; *Washington Post,* Oct. 7, 1888; *New York Herald,* Oct. 29, 1888.

27. Edwards, *Angels in the Machinery,* 63–64.

28. Calhoun, *From Bloody Shirt to Full Dinner Pail,* 101; Harrison, *Speeches,* 129–30; *Indianapolis Sun,* Aug. 1, 1888; *Indianapolis Journal,* Aug. 2, 1888.

29. Silber, *Romance of Reunion,* 97–98; Harrison, *Speeches,* 84.

30. Blight, *Race and Reunion,* 201–3; Silber, *Romance of Reunion,* 97.

31. Edwards, *Angels in the Machinery,* 61, 66–67; *New York Herald,* Aug. 4, 1888; *Chicago Tribune,* Aug. 4, 10, 1888; Jensen, *Winning of the Midwest,* 16; *Indianapolis Sun,* June 27, 1888.

32. Harrison, *Speeches,* 106; *Springfield (MA) Republican,* Sept. 30, 1888; Summers, *Party Games,* 52.

33. *New York Herald,* Aug. 4, 1888; *Chicago Tribune,* Aug. 14, 16, Oct. 9, 1888.

34. Harrison, *Speeches,* 34.

35. Harrison, *Speeches,* 140; *Chicago Tribune,* Sept. 23, 1888; Summers, *Party Games,* 37, 49.

36. Harrison, *Speeches,* 182–83; John Sleicher to Harrison, Oct. 26, 1888, Harrison Papers, vol. 44.

37. Edwards, *Angels in the Machinery,* 84; Richard J. Jensen, *Grass Roots Politics: Parties, Issues, and Voters, 1854–1983* (Westport, CT: Greenwood, 1983), 9; Tynes Bussey to James Clarkson, Sept. 15, 1888, James Clarkson Papers, Library of Congress, Washington, DC, 7; Charles Beardsley to James Clarkson, Sept. 21, 1888, Clarkson Papers, 12–13.

38. Dan Butterfield to Harrison, July 15, 1888, Harrison Papers, vol. 34; H. B. Stanley to Harrison, Aug. 2, 1888, Harrison Papers, vol. 35; Charles Hedges to William Henry

Smith, July 21, 1888, William Henry Smith Papers, 1800–96, Ohio Historical Society Archives, Columbus.

39. *Chicago Tribune,* Aug. 2, 1888; *Indianapolis Sun,* July 21, 1888; *New York Herald,* Oct. 6, 1888; *Harper's Weekly,* Sept. 1, 1888, 647.

40. *Indianapolis Sun,* June 30, 1888; *Chicago Tribune,* July 5, 1888.

41. *New York Herald,* Aug. 7, 1888; *Cleveland Plain Dealer,* July 4, 1888; *Saint Louis Dispatch,* Aug. 12, 22, Sept. 18, 1888; *Indianapolis Journal,* July 22, 1888; Blaine to Harrison, Nov. 4, 1888, Harrison Papers, vol. 45.

42. *Buffalo Express* and *Philadelphia American* as reprinted in *Indianapolis Journal,* Aug. 13, 1888; Calhoun, *Minority Victory,* 132, 182; Morgan, *From Hayes to McKinley,* 248, 271; McGerr, *Decline of Popular Politics,* 87–89.

43. There were numerous Democratic processions in Indianapolis in 1888. The *Saint Louis Dispatch* and the *Washington Post* reported on September 23 that the largest Democratic demonstration of the summer occurred the night before in which thousands of them marched, including African American, German Americans, Irish Americans, and first-time voters.

44. Calhoun, *Minority Victory,* 178–81.

45. John Quincy Adams won through the House of Representatives in 1825. Rutherford Hayes won in 1877 through an Electoral College Commission.

46. Walter Burnham, *Presidential Ballots, 1836–1892* (1955; repr., New York: Arno, 1976), 390–412.

3. THE PEN, THE PRESS, AND THE PLATFORM

1. *Cleveland Plain Dealer,* Oct. 1, 1896.

2. Edwards, *Angels in the Machinery,* 113.

3. Edwards, *Angels in the Machinery,* 113.

4. For more on Bryan, see Paul W. Glad, *The Trumpet Soundeth: William Jennings Bryan and His Democracy, 1896–1912* (Lincoln: Univ. of Nebraska Press, 1960); Paolo E. Coletta, *William Jennings Bryan,* 3 vols. (Lincoln: Univ. of Nebraska Press, 1964–69); Louis W. Koenig, *Bryan: A Political Biography of William Jennings Bryan* (New York: Putnam, 1971), Robert W. Cherny, *A Righteous Cause: The Life of William Jennings Bryan* (Boston: Little, Brown, 1985); Michael Kazin, *A Godly Hero: The Life of William Jennings Bryan* (New York: Knopf, 2006).

5. Gilbert C. Fite, "The Election of 1896," in *History of American Presidential Elections, 1848–1896,* ed. Arthur M. Schlesinger Jr., 4 vols. (New York: Chelsea House, 1971), 2:1814.

6. Fite, "Election of 1896," 1801–14.

7. For more on McKinley, see Margaret Leech, *In the Days of McKinley* (New York: Harper, 1959); H. Wayne Morgan, *William McKinley and His America* (Syracuse, NY: Syracuse Univ. Press, 1963); Lewis L. Gould, *The Presidency of William McKinley* (Lawrence: Univ. Press of Kansas, 1980); Judith Trent and Robert Friedenberg, *Political Campaign Communication: Principles and Practices,* 5th ed. (Lanham, MD: Rowman &

Littlefield, 2004); and Quentin R. Skrabec Jr., *William McKinley: Apostle of Protectionism* (New York: Algora, 2008).

8. For the most recent comprehensive analysis of the election of 1896, see Williams, *Realigning America.* See also Troy, *See How They Ran,* 102–7.

9. T. Bentley Mott, *Myron T. Herrick, Friend of France: An Autobiographical Biography* (Garden City, NY: Doubleday, 1929), 64; *Springfield (MA) Republican,* June 21, 1896. For the most recent analysis of McKinley's rhetorical abilities, see William D. Harpine, *From the Front-Porch to the Front Page: McKinley and Bryan in the 1896 Presidential Campaign* (College Station: Texas A&M Univ. Press, 2005), chaps. 3, 6, 7, and 9.

10. Fite, "Election of 1896."

11. Francis Russell, *The President Makers: From Mark Hanna to Joseph P. Kennedy* (Boston: Little, Brown, 1976), 4. Chapter 1 is a biography of Mark Hanna.

12. There is no record that they visited Garfield at his home.

13. Russell, *President Makers,* 10–25.

14. McGerr, *Decline of Popular Politics,* 140–42; Calhoun, *From Bloody Shirt to Full Dinner Pail,* 163.

15. John Lehman, *A Standard History of Stark County* (Chicago: Lewis, 1916), 289–312.

16. George B. Frease edited the *Repository* in 1896. He was the son of Joseph Frease, a local judge and McKinley's personal friend. When McKinley arrived in Canton in 1867, he succeeded Frease as a lawyer for the Belden & Frease firm. The firm became known as Belden & McKinley for the next two years until Belden's death. For the next twelve years, McKinley litigated in cases primarily presided over by Judge Frease. Another son of Judge Frease, Col. Harry Frease, served as one of the chief organizers of the processions to McKinley's home in 1896.

17. *Canton Repository,* Aug. 2, 1896.

18. *Chicago Tribune,* June 25, 1896; *Canton Repository,* June 25, Aug. 23, 1896; Skrabec, *William McKinley,* 144; *Toledo Blade,* June 18, 1896; *Cleveland Plain Dealer,* Oct. 22, 1896.

19. Williams, *Realigning America,* 134; Skrabec, *William McKinley,* 143; *Cleveland Plain Dealer,* Sept. 17, 1896; *Canton Repository,* June 18, 25, 1896; *Chicago Evening Post,* Sept. 11, 1896; *Chicago Tribune,* June 25, 1896.

20. Williams, *Realigning America,* 132; *Chicago Tribune,* July 13, 1896; *Toledo Blade,* Aug. 6, 1896; Skrabec, *William McKinley,* 143.

21. *Toledo Blade,* Sept. 12, 1896; *Chicago Tribune,* June 20, 1896.

22. *Cleveland Plain Dealer,* June 20, Oct. 14, 18, 22, 24, 1896.

23. *Cleveland Plain Dealer,* Sept. 12, 1896.

24. *Canton Repository,* Sept. 24, 1896; *Cleveland Plain Dealer,* Oct. 9, 1896.

25. *Cleveland Plain Dealer,* Oct. 9, 1896.

26. *Cleveland Plain Dealer,* Oct. 4, 9, 1896; *Canton Repository,* Oct. 11, Nov. 5, 1896.

27. *Indianapolis Sun,* Oct. 14, 1896; *Chicago Tribune,* July 4, 1896; *Canton Repository,* Oct. 28, 1896.

28. *Springfield (MA) Republican,* June 26, July 16, 1896.

29. *Cleveland Plain Dealer,* July 14, 1896; *Indianapolis Sentinel,* July 15, 1896; *Canton Repository,* July 16, 1896; *Chicago Tribune,* July 16, 1896.

30. *Cleveland Plain Dealer,* July 16, 1896.

31. *Cleveland Plain Dealer,* July 16, 1896.

32. *Chicago Tribune,* July 4, 1896.

33. *Chicago Tribune,* June 27, 1896.

34. *Cleveland Plain Dealer,* Sept. 12, 1896.

35. *Cleveland Plain Dealer,* June 28, 1896.

36. *Canton Repository,* June 21, 1896; *Cleveland Plain Dealer,* July 4, Aug. 19, 20, Sept. 29, 1896.

37. *Cleveland Plain Dealer,* July 4, 13, Aug. 14, 1896.

38. *Cleveland Plain Dealer,* Aug. 1, 1896; *Chicago Tribune,* July 18, 1896.

39. *Cleveland Plain Dealer,* Sept. 28, Oct. 15, 1896.

40. *Chicago Tribune,* June 28, 1896.

41. *Canton Repository,* Oct. 25, 1896.

42. *Cleveland Plain Dealer,* Aug. 31, 1896.

43. Troy, *See How They Ran,* 106; *Canton Repository,* July 26, Aug. 2, Oct. 8, 1896; *Cleveland Plain Dealer,* Sept. 12, Oct. 4, 15, 22, 1896.

44. *Indianapolis Sun,* June 24, 1896; *Cleveland Plain Dealer,* Oct. 3, 12, 1896.

45. Williams, *Realigning America,* 150; *Canton Repository,* Aug. 20, 1896.

4. BETWEEN CANTON AND MARION

Portions of this chapter were first published in "'Just Call Me Bill': William Taft Brings Spectacle Politics to the Midwest," *Studies in Midwestern History* 2, no. 10 (Oct. 2016): 113–38. Reused with permission.

1. *New York Times,* Sept. 29, 1908; *Fargo (ND) Daily News,* Sept. 29, 1908; *New York Herald,* Sept. 29, 1908.

2. *New York Times,* Sept. 29, 1908; *Cincinnati Enquirer,* Sept. 29, 1908; *Chattanooga Daily Times,* Sept. 29, 1908; *New York Herald,* Sept. 29, 1908.

3. Troy outlines this question in *See How They Ran,* 120.

4. Troy, *See How They Ran,* 108, 117.

5. Marvin R. Weisbord, *Campaigning for President: A New Look at the Road to the White House* (Washington, DC: Public Affairs, 1964), 78; J. Rogers Hollingsworth, *The Whirligig of Politics: The Democracy of Cleveland and Bryan* (Chicago: Univ. of Chicago Press, 1963), 178–79; Troy, *See How They Ran,* 110, 111.

6. Edwards, *Angels in the Machinery,* 154–56.

7. Troy, *See How They Ran,* 113–17; *Review of Reviews* (Nov. 1904): 522; *Saint Louis Dispatch,* Nov. 1, 1904; *New York Press,* July 30, 1904.

8. *New York Times,* Sept. 7, 22, 1908; Troy, *See How They Ran,* 121, 124; *The Nation,* Sept. 10, 1908; *Washington Times,* Aug. 23, 1908.

9. Troy, *See How They Ran,* 126; *New York Times,* May 24, 1908.

10. It is a considerably different endeavor to measure crime on the campaign trail than in a front porch setting because stumping involves candidates visiting locations for a few minutes or hours, while the front porch campaign puts one city at risk for

a consistent, extended period. Yet with this assassination attempt, it is safe to argue that some crimes were certainly committed in places where the candidates appeared for stump speeches during the early twentieth century.

11. *New York Times,* Apr. 28, 1908.

12. Troy, *See How They Ran,* 128–31.

13. *New York Times,* Aug. 5, 1916; Troy, *See How They Ran,* 135.

14. *Chicago Tribune,* Aug. 9, 1916.

15. Troy, *See How They Ran,* 138–39.

16. *New York Times,* Oct. 5, 1916; Troy, *See How They Ran,* 140.

5. PHONOGRAPHS, FRIENDLY REPORTERS, AND THE
FINAL FRONT PORCH CAMPAIGN

1. *Los Angeles Times,* Aug. 14, 31, 1920; *New York Tribune,* Aug. 14, 1920.

2. For some of the best literature on Harding's front porch campaign in 1920, see Wesley M. Bagby, *The Road to Normalcy: The Presidential Campaign and the Election of 1920* (Baltimore: John Hopkins Univ. Press, 1962); Andrew Sinclair, *The Available Man: The Life behind the Masks of Warren Gamaliel Harding* (New York: Macmillan, 1965), 160–64; Robert K. Murray, *The Harding Era: Warren G. Harding and His Administration* (Minneapolis: Univ. of Minnesota Press, 1969), 45–58; Randolph C. Downes, *The Rise of Warren Gamaliel Harding, 1865–1920* (Columbus: Ohio State Univ. Press, 1970), 452–86; Schlesinger, *History of American Presidential Elections;* Eugene H. Roseboom, *A History of Presidential Elections, from George Washington to Jimmy Carter,* 4th ed. (New York: Macmillan, 1979); and John W. Dean, *Warren G. Harding* (New York: Times Books, 2004). For the latest interpretation of the summer of 1920 in Marion, see Phillip G. Payne, *Dead Last: The Public Memory of Warren G. Harding's Scandalous Legacy* (Athens: Ohio Univ. Press, 2009), 20–47.

3. John A. Morello, *Selling the President, 1920: Albert D. Lasker, Advertising, and the Election of Warren G. Harding* (Westport, CT: Praeger, 2001), 49–59.

4. According to Philip Payne, civic boosterism is promoting the community through community-driven activities and is rooted in consistent community harmony and the economic growth that promoted it. People engaged in business not only for profit but also for the good of the community as part of their civic responsibility as local leaders. See *Dead Last,* 20–47.

5. Russell, *President Makers,* 193, 206, 209; Frances Russell, *The Shadow of Blooming Grove: Warren G. Harding in His Times* (New York: McGraw-Hill, 1968), 241.

6. Donald R. McCoy, "The Election of 1920," in *History of American Presidential Elections, 1848–1896,* ed. Arthur M. Schlesinger Jr., 4 vols. (New York: Chelsea House, 1971), 3:2351–53.

7. McCoy, "The Election of 1920," 2352, 2353, 2357–58; Roseboom, *Presidential Elections,* 394.

8. For the standard works on Harding, see Russell, *Shadow of Blooming Grove;* Murray, *Harding Era;* Downes, *Rise of Warren Gamaliel Harding;* Eugene P. Trani

and David L. Wilson, *The Presidency of Warren G. Harding* (Lawrence: Univ. Press of Kansas, 1977); Dean, *Warren G. Harding;* and Payne, *Dead Last.*

9. Downes, *Rise of Warren Gamaliel Harding,* 248; *Chicago Tribune,* July 8, 11, 17, 1920.

10. Elizabeth Reid to Will Hays, July 2, 1920, folder 4, box 13, Will Hays Papers, Indiana State Library, Indianapolis.

11. Burt Cady to Will Hays, July 15, 1920, folder 1, box 14, Hays Papers.

12. Downes, *Rise of Warren Gamaliel Harding,* 462.

13. Downes, *Rise of Warren Gamaliel Harding,* 461, 462.

14. Murray, *Harding Era,* 50, 250; Downes, *Rise of Warren Gamaliel Harding,* 460, 463.

15. Downes, *Rise of Warren Gamaliel Harding,* 461, 462; *Chicago Tribune,* July 1, 1920; McCoy, "The Election of 1920," 2372.

16. *Marion Star,* June 16, 1920.

17. *Chicago Tribune,* June 17, 1920.

18. *Los Angeles Times,* July 25, 26, 1920.

19. *Philadelphia Inquirer,* July 1, 1920, folder 4, box 13, Hays Papers; L. W. Henley to Hays, July 10, 1920, folder 5, Hays Papers.

20. *Marion Star,* June 15, 1920.

21. *Marion Star,* June 23, 1920; *Chicago Tribune,* July 20, 1920.

22. *Marion Star,* July 21, 1920.

23. *Chicago Tribune,* July 18, 1920.

24. Downes, *Rise of Warren Gamaliel Harding,* 455; Murray, *Harding Era,* 50, 52; Sinclair, *Available Man,* 164.

25. Murray, *Harding Era,* 50, 51; Downes, *Rise of Warren Gamaliel Harding,* 454, 459; Preston Wentworth to C. B. Miller, Aug. 13, 1920, folder 3, box 15, Hays Papers; W. H. Hamilton to Hays, July 27, 1920, folder 3, box 14, Hays Papers.

26. *Memphis Commercial Appeal,* Aug. 4, 1920; *Chicago Tribune,* Aug. 7, 1920.

27. McCoy, "The Election of 1920," 2372; Troy, *See How They Ran,* 277.

28. *Memphis Commercial Appeal,* Aug. 4, 1920.

29. *Los Angeles Times,* Aug. 24, 1920.

30. Downes, *Rise of Warren Gamaliel Harding,* 472; *Los Angeles Times,* July 29, 1920; *New York Tribune,* Sept. 3, 1920; *Chicago Tribune,* Sept. 3, 1920.

31. *Chicago Tribune,* Aug. 22, 1920.

32. *Chicago Tribune,* Aug. 25, 1920.

33. David Pietrusza, *1920: The Year of the Six Presidents* (New York: Carroll & Graf, 2007), 341.

34. *Los Angeles Times,* Aug. 24, 1920.

35. *Memphis Commercial Appeal,* Aug. 19, 1920; *New York Tribune,* Sept. 5, 1920; *Chicago Tribune,* June 14, 1920.

36. Newspaper clipping, folder 5, box 14, Hays Papers; Will H. Hays, *Memoirs* (Garden City, NY: Doubleday, 1955), 265.

37. Downes, *Rise of Warren Gamaliel Harding,* 476.

38. *Chicago Tribune,* Sept. 11, 1920; Downes, *Rise of Warren Gamaliel Harding,* 476.

39. Pietrusza, *1920,* 349; *Los Angeles Times,* Sept. 19, 1920.

40. Downes, *Rise of Warren Gamaliel Harding,* 481.

41. *Los Angeles Times,* Aug. 25, 1920.

42. *Los Angeles Times,* Aug. 30, 1920.

43. *Los Angeles Times,* Aug. 14, 1920.

44. *Los Angeles Times,* Sept. 21, 1920.

45. *Marion Star,* June 19, 1920.

46. Newspaper clipping, folder 1, box 15, Hays Papers.

47. Newspaper clipping, folder 1, box 15, Hays Papers.

48. *Chicago Tribune,* July 16, 1920; *Marion Star,* July 22, 1920.

49. *Chicago Tribune,* July 22, Aug. 6, 1920.

50. *Chicago Tribune,* Aug. 26, 28, 1920.

51. *Los Angeles Times,* Oct. 2, 19, 1920.

52. Newspaper clipping, folder 5, box 16, Hays Papers.

53. Downes, *Rise of Warren Gamaliel Harding,* 485.

54. Downes, *Rise of Warren Gamaliel Harding,* 486.

Index